Horse Racing's Holy Grail

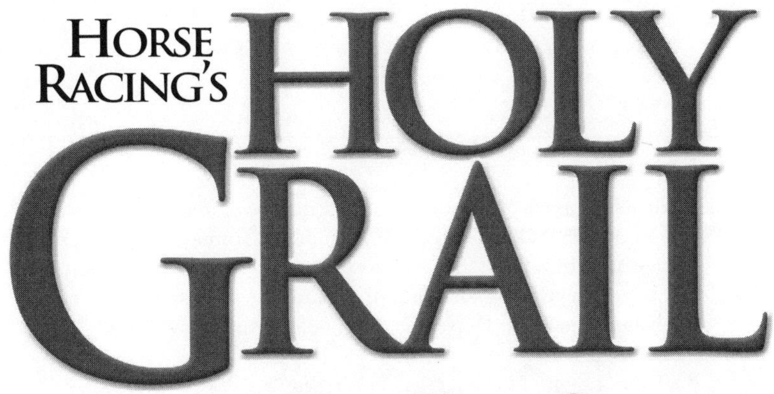

The Epic Quest for the Kentucky Derby

Steve Haskin

Lexington, Kentucky

Library of Congress Control Number: 2001098719

ISBN 1-58150-076-9

Printed in the United States
First Edition: April 2002

Distributed to the trade by
National Book Network
4720-A Boston Way
Lanham, MD 20706
1.800.462.6420

a division of
The Blood-Horse, Inc.
PUBLISHERS SINCE 1916

Contents

To my beloved Joan and Mandy,
who are the roses in my life
and inspire every word I write.

INTRODUCTION

Atop the World

Within the hallowed halls of Churchill Downs appear the names of 127 horses who have ascended the summit of the Kentucky Derby — the K2 of Thoroughbred racing. Like the formidable mountain of the Himalayas, the Derby is not for the meek, and it has no mercy on those who fail. Nowhere do you hear even a whisper of the 1,578 horses whose attempt at immortality proved futile. And that doesn't include the thousands upon thousands more who set off on the adventure but failed even to reach the base of the mountain.

There are no rules and no marked paths when it comes to the Kentucky Derby. As anyone who has ever wagered on the Derby, ridden a horse in the Derby, saddled a horse in the Derby, or owned a horse in the Derby will tell you, more questions surround the Run for the Roses than answers.

Why did only four trainers — D. Wayne Lukas, Bob Baffert, Nick Zito, and Charlie Whittingham — win ten of the fourteen runnings of the Derby from 1986 to 1999?

Why have all the remaining Derby-winning trainers since 1986 — Jack Van Berg, Carl Nafzger, Lynn Whiting, Mack Miller, Neil Drysdale, and John T. Ward Jr. — been veteran horsemen who paid their dues with a solid record in major races?

Why do relatively unknown trainers come to Churchill Downs year after year with winners of the Blue Grass Stakes, Santa Anita Derby, Wood Memorial, Arkansas Derby, Florida Derby, and Louisiana Derby, only to finish far up the track? In the nineties, long-since-forgotten trainers such as Tom Arnemann, Wayne Catalano, Ben Glass Jr., Dallas Keen, Jim Ryerson, Randy Winick, Bret Thomas, and Chuck Turco won at least one of the aforementioned stakes only to have their horse finish off the board in the Kentucky Derby. In fact, their average finish in the Derby was eleventh. None of them have returned since.

Why have two former Quarter Horse trainers — Lukas and Baffert — and an Italian from the streets of New York City — Zito — managed to win or place

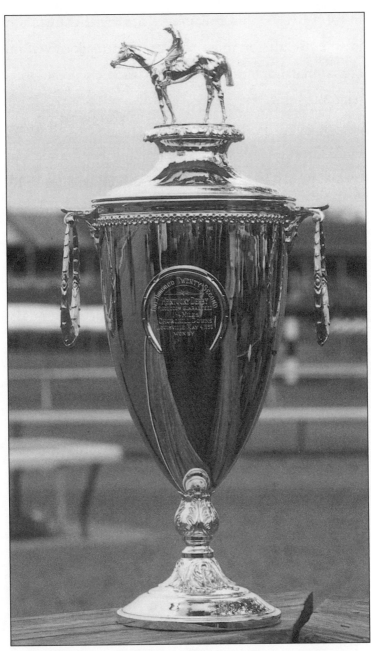

The Derby trophy seldom goes to the faint of heart.

in forty-five Triple Crown races among them when it is so difficult for most top trainers to get even an occasional horse to compete in racing's prestigious triad?

I am about to attempt to answer these and many more questions regarding the greatest two minutes in sports. And even if I don't, it still should be a fun ride. The secrets to the Kentucky Derby have remained hidden for more than 125 years, and as far as I know, there is no Hydra guarding them; there is no Pharaoh's curse on those who dare attempt to unlock their mysteries. Maybe there will be a giant runaway boulder or a few poison darts to contend with, but isn't it worth the risk to uncover such treasured secrets? Heck, even Lukas, Baffert, and Zito don't really know how they do it. Of the eight Derbys they've won among them, they've basically gone about it differently each time. Where one way has worked for some of their horses, it's failed for others that were equally, if not more, talented.

I will examine the pitfalls and traps young, inexperienced trainers fall into; try to explain why no two-year-old champion since 1979 nor Breeders' Cup Juvenile winner has been able to capture the Derby; why no favorite won the Derby for twenty-one years, from 1980 until 2000; how the road to Louisville has changed dramatically over the years; what kind of horse it takes, mentally and physically, to win the Derby; what signs to look for in a young two-year-old; how to conquer Churchill Downs; why it's more difficult now to win the Derby than in past years; and much more. To do this, I will venture into the core of the Derby itself, pulling out personal experiences, interactions with trainers, historical trends, and anecdotes along the way.

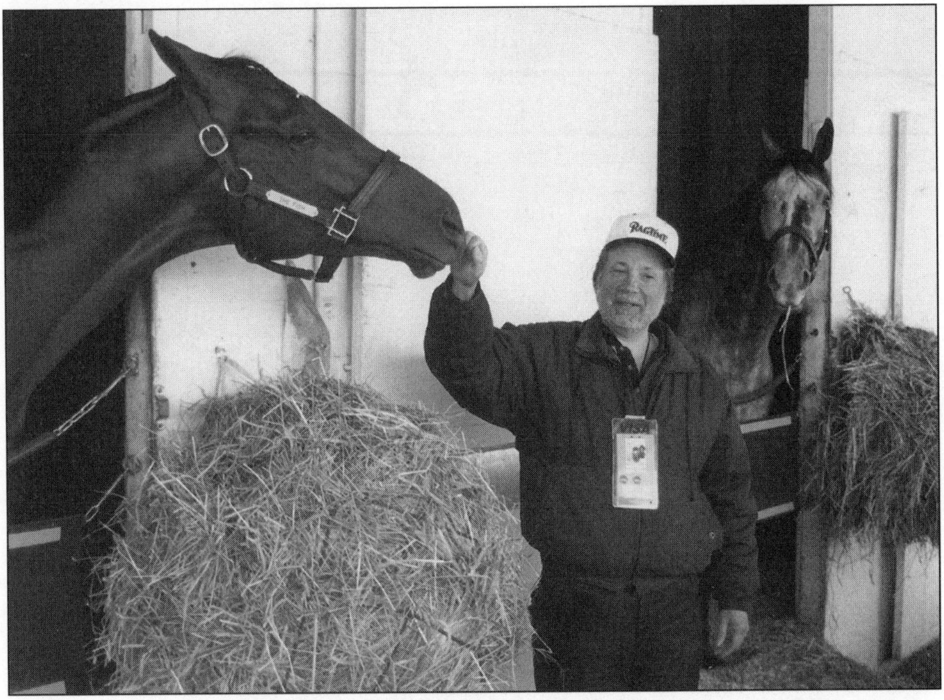

The author visits with Real Quiet, his sleeper pick of 1998. Silver Charm, the 1997 winner, looks on.

Now let's be honest right from the start. My record betting the Kentucky Derby can be described at best as pitiful, although I will boast here and now of hitting the 2001 exacta of Monarchos over Invisible Ink, which paid $1,229, the biggest ticket I have ever cashed. Bragging is one of the fringe benefits of writing a book, and, besides, I don't want to start off looking totally inept at what I'm about to preach. But I must admit, my betting foibles on

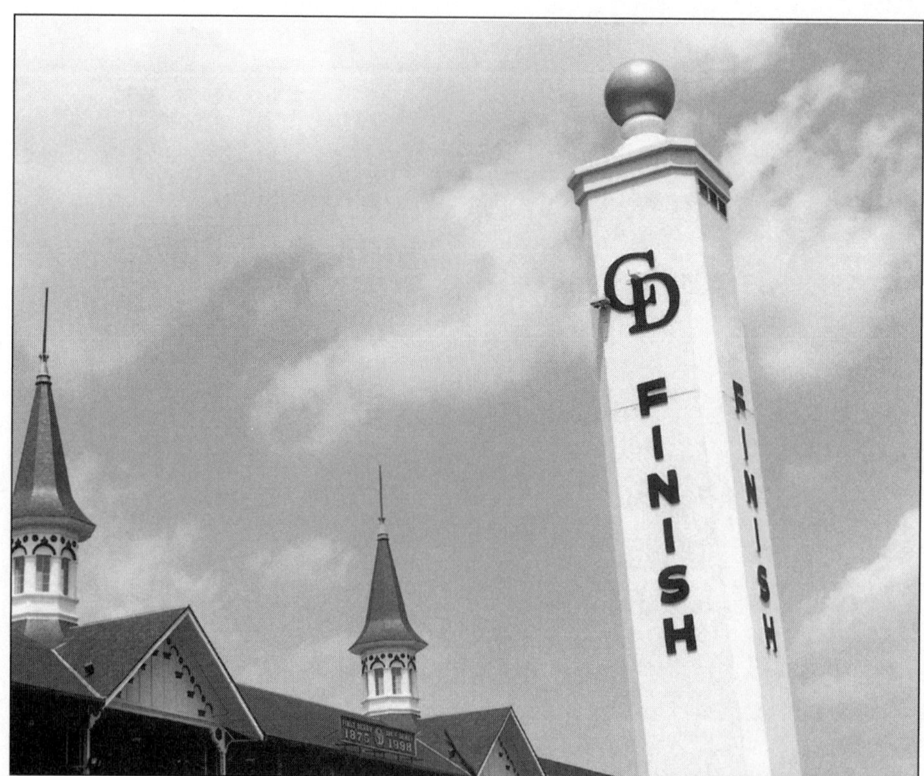

The elusive finish line — sought by many, attained by few.

Derby Day are caused mainly by indecisiveness and cowardice — two flaws that will eat away at you and your wallet, leaving nothing behind but the desire for self-inflicted punishment. Understand, however, I am not a big bettor. Frankly, I don't like losing money on horses, and the Derby is one race where you can't be afraid to lose. You must make a commitment. But each year, the coward in me surfaces and causes me to protect myself with some of the most idiotic saver bets imaginable. So even in years when I hit the winner, I'm fortunate if I break even or win a few dollars. In 2001 I handicapped strictly off works and appearance instead of form and finally got lucky.

All I will say about my betting exploits in the Derby is that I loved Fusaichi Pegasus in 2000, having ranked him as my No. 1 Derby horse in mid-February, before he even ran in a stakes; I bet on Charismatic in the race *before* the 1999 Derby; and I selected Real Quiet as one of the sleepers of the '98 Derby based on his works and appearance. My total winnings those years: zero. Whether it was due to the fact that I never bet on favorites or have a slight tendency to shy away from horses who don't meet the desired dosage index of 4.00 or under, which we'll get into later, the net total still was zero. But you know the old saying: Do as I say, not as I do.

I am about to begin the adventure, armed with nothing more than thirty-odd years of watching and studying the Derby. I've gotten to know many of the top trainers on a more than professional level and have stored away their many "off the record" and "between you and me" comments. I've attacked the Derby from the trenches, being on the Churchill Downs backstretch two weeks before the race, at 5:30 each morning. I've spoken to trainers with Derby hopefuls beginning in January each year for the last eight years, for the weekly "Derby Watch" and "Derby Report" features in the *Daily Racing Form* and *The Blood-Horse* magazine, respectively. I have witnessed firsthand all the Derby dos and don'ts, and heard all the second-guessing afterward that results from the doing the don'ts or not doing the dos.

I've watched Bob Baffert have his first Derby victory snatched away from him, as though plucked right out of his soul, and I listened to the twelve months of torment that followed. I also was there for the family celebrations that followed his two victories. I have shared many a bottle of wine with Nick Zito and often witnessed the spirit of the Derby emanate from his very being as he spoke of the race with almost divine reverence. I have had Wayne Lukas pour out his heart and guts to me at 4:30, the morning after Grindstone's victory when a special moment — winning the Derby for William T. Young — was tarnished by an earlier assault in the *Louisville Courier-Journal,* in which fellow trainers implied he was more of a marketing man than a horseman. I also flew with Lukas and Thunder Gulch and Timber Country from Louisville to New York following their respective victories in the Derby and Preakness, and with Baffert and Silver Charm, joining them on their quest for the Triple Crown.

A good deal of what follows is their story. They have been able to reach out and hold the elusive moonbeam in their hand more than once. But this is also the story of those who have tried and failed. Some have persevered their whole lives and never come close. Others have had it within their grasp, only to see it slip through their fingers. They, and most every other horseman in America, can only dream of what it feels like to stand under the shadow of the Twin Spires and savor the intoxicating fragrance of the blanket of roses as it is draped over their horse's withers. They can only dream of holding that treasured trophy up to the heavens in the knowledge that their name will be immortalized in Derby and racing lore for all time.

So, if you want to know how to go about experiencing those magical moments, or just enjoy the year's bragging rights that accompany betting the Derby winner, then sit back, kick off your shoes, and enter the world of the Kentucky Derby. A good deal of what you are about to read is intended as lighthearted fun as we explore this wondrous realm through every crevice and corridor. But who knows, maybe deep within its recesses we will uncover the secret to riches and glory that in the past existed only in dreams.

Steve Haskin

Hamilton Square, New Jersey 2001

CHAPTER

They Just Don't Get It

When people ask me how many Kentucky Derbys I've covered or even witnessed, I'm almost embarrassed to tell them ten, because I know they are expecting me to start spinning yarns about Native Dancer's troubled trip or Bill Shoemaker's misjudging the finish line on Gallant Man. I feel the urge to apologize that I experienced my previous Derbys from Mercer County, New Jersey, at an annual Derby party that included a Calcutta pool.

Now I've *seen* thirty-four Derbys, but not being fond of big crowds, I was content to watch them on television until I became a full-time writer for the *Daily Racing Form* and received my first Derby assignment in 1992. I had written free-lance for many racing publications since 1976, but remained imprisoned in the library at the *Form*, where I had been toiling for the previous twenty years. It was only a coup against the monarchy by several of the editors that freed me from captivity and thrust me onto the Derby scene.

So here I was, covering my first Kentucky Derby, engulfed by the phenomenon known as Arazimania. In witnessing this unique experience firsthand, I came to realize why no favorite had won the Derby since 1979. It was Arazi who opened my eyes to all the other false favorites over the years and prepared me for the drought that would continue until Fusaichi Pegasus broke the ignominious streak in 2000.

While awaiting the arrival of the French wonder horse, I decided to explore some of the little-known elements of the Derby that had always fascinated me. One was the setup on the Churchill Downs backstretch, in which Derby horses graze inside a chain-link fence that separates them from passersby and residents of Longfield Avenue. Imagine, I thought, what some of these folks, who have been living across the street for twenty, thirty, or even forty years, might have to say about seeing so many great horses right from their front porch. The first person whose comments I solicited was a toothless old guy, to whom I am grateful for putting things in their proper perspective. He looked at me square in the eye and replied to my inquiry, "I ain't no racehorse person, but I'm fer 'em, I ain' agin 'em." Goodbye New Jersey, hello Kentucky.

To those who were not part of the pandemonium that swept through Louisville in 1992, Arazi was the red chestnut whirlwind that practically blew the Twin Spires off the Churchill Downs roof with his spectacular move in the 1991 Breeders' Cup Juvenile after a championship campaign in France. Breaking from the disadvantageous fourteen post, and making his first start ever on dirt, this pocket-sized missile, in the blink of an eye, hurtled through the entire field in one of the most amazing displays of speed and acceleration ever witnessed. Who can forget listening to race-caller Tom Durkin as he realized the anticipated stretch battle between Arazi and California speedster Bertrando, who had led all the way, was not going to happen. "And Arazi runs right by him!" he bellowed in disbelief. "Bertrando is stunned by the move of Arazi!"

The second he crossed the finish line, five lengths ahead of Bertrando, Arazi became the hottest Kentucky Derby favorite in memory. For six months this dubious title attached itself to the horse like a barnacle. After all, no favorite had won the Derby since Spectacular Bid thirteen years earlier. Americans had themselves a white-hot Derby favorite, but no way of knowing what he was doing back home in the equine Shangri-la known as Chantilly. I was able to get periodic reports through the *Form*'s artist Pierre Bellocq, better known as Peb, who phoned trainer François Boutin, feeding him my questions and interpreting his answers.

Winter passed, and Derby fever began to escalate with the blossoming of the forsythias and crocuses. In America it was like the Filipinos awaiting the return of MacArthur. Racing fans were desperate for a savior to free them from the bonds of mediocrity. You see, we were all spoiled from the heroes of the super seventies. Although the country had seen some sensational Thoroughbreds in recent years, including Alysheba and the great rivalry between Sunday Silence and Easy Goer, folks were getting itchy for a Triple Crown winner — one who possessed the surge of electricity that could jolt the grandstands of Churchill Downs, Pimlico, and Belmont Park. They were convinced they had found him in the little chestnut colt with the crooked blaze and winged feet.

But there was one little detail that people were overlooking. Arazi had no chance to win the Derby. He was destined to be another of the many false favorites on the first Saturday in May. People were thinking

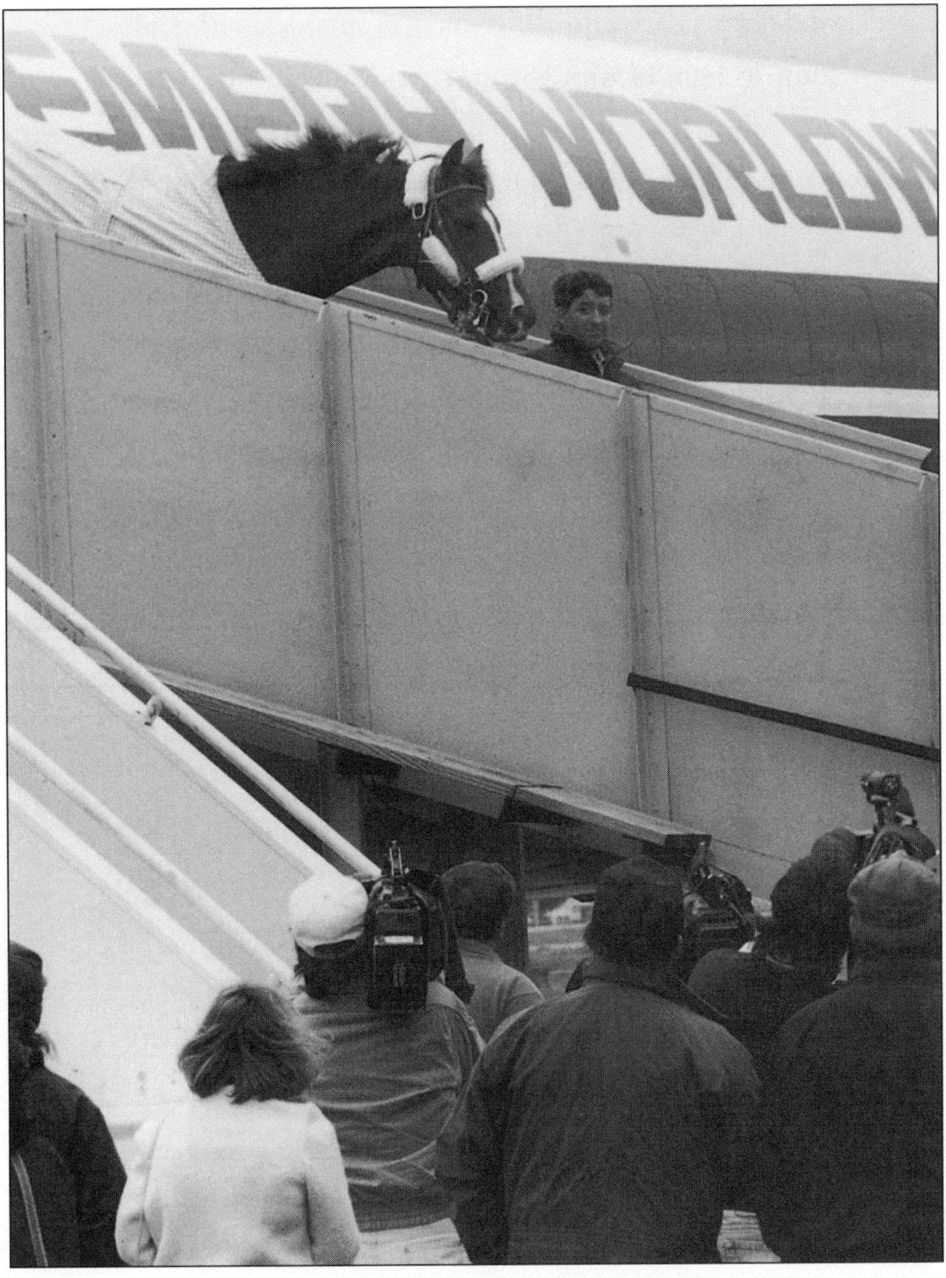

Arazi's arrival in Louisville generated a media frenzy.

with their hearts instead of their brains, and although I am usually in that group, I wanted to shout, "You just don't get it."

Not only had owner Allen Paulson sold a half-interest in Arazi to Sheikh Mohammed al Maktoum of Dubai, causing a clash of two worlds and differences of opinion, but Arazi had also undergone knee surgery to remove bone chips after the Breeders' Cup, a procedure many around him felt wasn't necessary. Arazi made one start before the 1992 Kentucky Derby, a ridiculously easy victory in the one-mile Prix Omnium at Saint-Cloud over soft going. Off of this one easy score, he was supposed to win the Derby, despite never having been farther than a mile and a sixteenth, despite having had knee surgery, and despite having two jockeys with diverse riding styles and two owners with very different philosophies on what their goals were and how to achieve them.

I'll never forget the day Arazi arrived in Louisville. As a fan, I desperately wanted him to win and was hoping maybe he was a superhorse of such magnitude he could overcome everything he had going against him. But that hope was slim, and I knew it. It was a cold, miserable Sunday, but in the air there was a sense of anticipation that I had never felt before and have never felt since. It was as if the Pope were arriving in Kentucky to bless the Sport of Kings. The ethereal had replaced the logical. But who cared? Arazi was coming.

The colt was scheduled to arrive at Butler Field in Louisville at 2:00 in the afternoon. At 1:30 Bob Bailey, head of security for Churchill Downs, looked out his office window at the old J.J. Carter moving and storage building across the street. That would be the makeshift quarantine station, where Arazi would call

Hordes of media also awaited Arazi at Churchill Downs.

home for the next forty-eight hours. Bailey called stall superintendent Mike Hargrove, who told him the plane was on time. By 1:45 Bailey hadn't heard back from Hargrove and was getting antsy. He tried to contact Louisville police officer Boone Pike, who was in charge of coordinating traffic and blocking off nearby Rodman Avenue.

Still no word. Bailey had to do something to keep himself occupied, so he called Lieutenant Don Burbrink and Officer Tom Coin, Louisville police officers who work for Churchill, to go over last-minute instructions on how the barricades would be set up. Bailey then took a nail clipper from his pocket and nervously began to clean his fingernails.

"What are we forgetting, Ron?" he asked an associate, Ron Gnagie. "I'm sure we're forgetting to do something. I've been going over and over everything in my mind."

At 2:40 Bailey learned the van still hadn't left the airport. "Let's get that horse here already," he said. Finally at 3:00, the phone rang. Bailey quickly picked it up and said nothing. After hanging up, he called out to the main communications room, "Call dispatch. Tell Boone they're on their way."

Meanwhile, the crowd outside the quarantine facili-

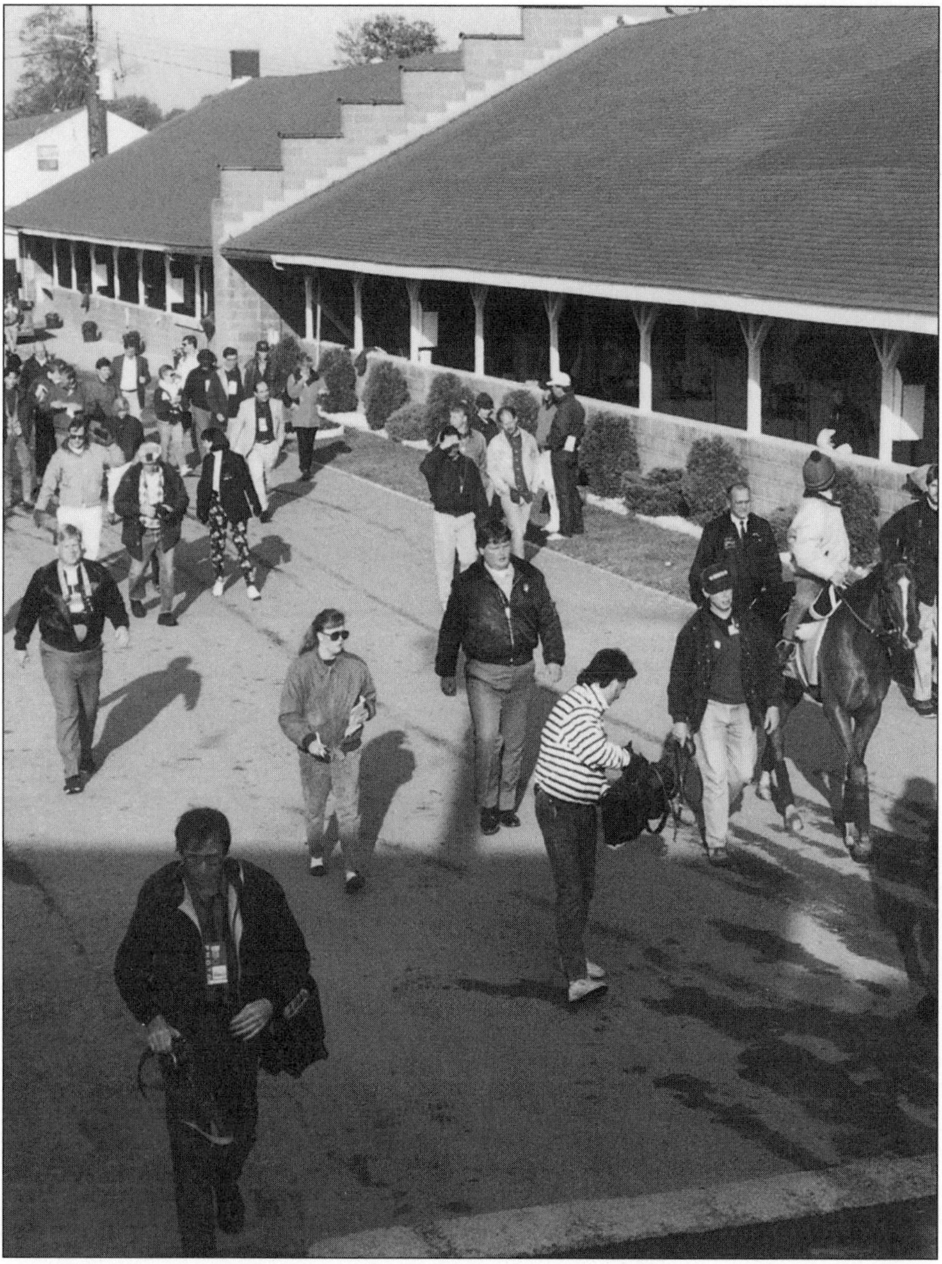

Arazi had plenty of followers on the way to the racetrack.

ty had begun to build. By now, the seventy or so reporters and photographers were chilled to the bone. The entrance to the building was guarded by two uniformed Murray guards from the private security firm hired by Churchill. Soon, the crowd swelled as locals began to gather. People driving down Central Avenue looked quizzically at this unusual gathering. Bailey stood by the curb, peering up the street. The latest report was that the van had just exited the Waterson Expressway. At 3:35 Bailey announced what everyone had been waiting hours to hear: "They're here."

Then it all happened so fast. The van made the turn onto the side street and pulled up outside the quarantine facility. The doors slid open, and there in all its glory was the chestnut face with the crooked blaze America had been waiting to see again for the past six months. Arazi had arrived. The most exciting week I have ever spent at a racetrack was about to begin.

I mention all this to show what can happen when the frenzy of the Derby is intensified by the delirium that accompanies the presence of a superstar. In this case, it was a superstar that was ill prepared to handle the grueling mile and a quarter of the Derby. When Arazi went to the track for the first time after being released from quarantine, people lined up six and seven deep behind the rail to get a glimpse of him. Every one of Arazi's baths was witnessed by humongous crowds, and when the colt went to the track, he was trailed by a mass of humanity that resembled the Hebrews following Moses out of Egypt.

For a brief moment during the race, it looked as if the fairy tale were going to come true. Arazi once again made a breathtaking move, this time well out in the middle of the track, that carried him from seventeenth to third. It literally took my breath away. The grandstand shook, and my hands trembled as I attempted in vain to keep my binoculars steady. God, I was wrong all along, and I loved it. This was indeed

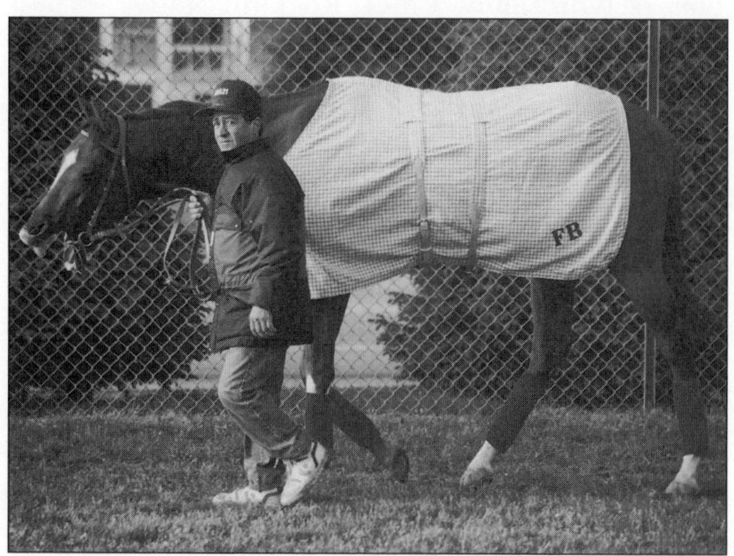

Arazi — a mere horse after all.

the second coming. Pegasus was sprouting wings right before my eyes. But then, just like that, reality hit with the force of a sledgehammer, knocking all the dreamers square on the head. Arazi's explosion fizzled. The little French colt who had captivated two hemispheres like no other horse in history was mortal after all. He retreated to eighth and also from the minds of those who had worshiped him.

What is the moral of the Arazi story? When you look at the statistics regarding Derby favorites and you see that only one favorite has won in the past twenty-two years, don't make too much out of it. In retrospect, would you consider horses like Althea, Air Forbes Won, Snow Chief, Rockhill Native, Proud Appeal, and Marfa (and his entrymates Balboa Native and Total Departure) legitimate Derby favorites? Or even legitimate mile and a quarter horses?

We know now that 1990 Derby favorite Mister Frisky ran in the race with a grapefruit-sized lump in his throat that would almost cost him his life. We know now that Demons Begone, wearing front bandages and having built his reputation as a three-year-old solely at Oaklawn Park, had no chance in the 1987 Derby after bleeding profusely and pulling up down the backstretch. We know now that Indian

Charlie (1998) was at a disadvantage with only four career starts, and that Unbridled's Song (1996) was fighting a losing battle, suffering from a quarter crack and wearing cumbersome egg-bar shoes. We know now that General Challenge (1999) did not have the mental fortitude to handle a race like the Derby. And, we know now that Point Given (2001) was being bothered by a nagging foot ailment during Derby Week.

In short, we know now that it is easy to make a horse the favorite when he doesn't deserve to be and that sometimes legitimate favorites are simply doomed from the start because of unforeseen circumstances. The dreadful record of Derby favorites over the past two decades has nothing to do with horses at all. It has to do with people. We are the culprits, not the favorites to which we bestow an honor that is now looked upon with such ambiguity.

In 2000 we put the grand-looking Fusaichi Pegasus up on a pedestal and made him the 2-1 favorite in the Derby. After he won like the wonder horse we had hoped for, many turned on him for being over-hyped and underraced, mainly because he had the audacity to lose the Preakness and miss the Belmont with a foot injury. The animosity grew after the horse's breeding rights were sold to Coolmore Stud, giving him a value estimated at sixty million to seventy million dollars. Whatever the reasons for his shortened career, the fact is we crowned a king and then attempted to dethrone him when he failed to serve us in the manner we wanted. Perhaps one day the racing gods will grant us the ultimate hero we've been searching for. Perhaps when they feel we deserve him.

CHAPTER

The Search Begins

Contrary to what many people think, the riches of the Thoroughbred world are not found under glass at Tiffany's or on display at Gucci or in the showroom at the nearest Jaguar dealership. They often are discovered hidden away on a shelf at K-Mart or in the back of a local Chevy lot. All you have to do is shop around for them, and then get incredibly lucky. "Incredibly" probably isn't strong enough, but it's the only word that comes to mind at the moment.

On the hunt for a Kentucky Derby winner, here's basically what you're dealing with: you can go to Keeneland and pay four million dollars for Fusaichi Pegasus or you can break open your piggy bank, take about nine percent of that amount — $355,400 to be exact — and buy Seattle Slew, Spectacular Bid, Genuine Risk, Silver Charm, Sunday Silence, Unbridled, Bold Forbes, Foolish Pleasure, Thunder Gulch, Go for Gin, Real

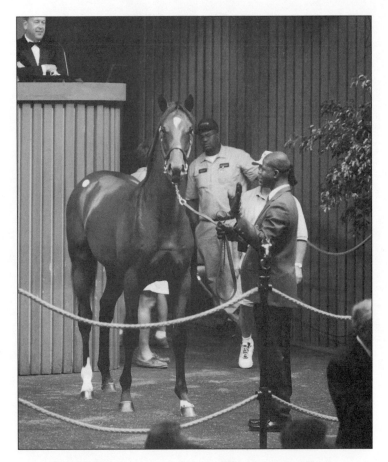

Fusaichi Pegasus cost four million as a yearling...

Quiet, Lil E. Tee, and Canonero II. That's right, for that amount you get all of them — thirteen Kentucky Derby winners for an average price of $27,338. Even if you're able to scrape up a mere twenty thousand bucks, you still could have bought any one of six of the aforementioned Derby winners and in all instances but one, gone home with change.

Remember, Thoroughbred racing may still be the Sport of Kings in some ways, but the most common of arses often sit upon its throne.

Now that we've established a Kentucky Derby winner can be purchased at any price, the next logical

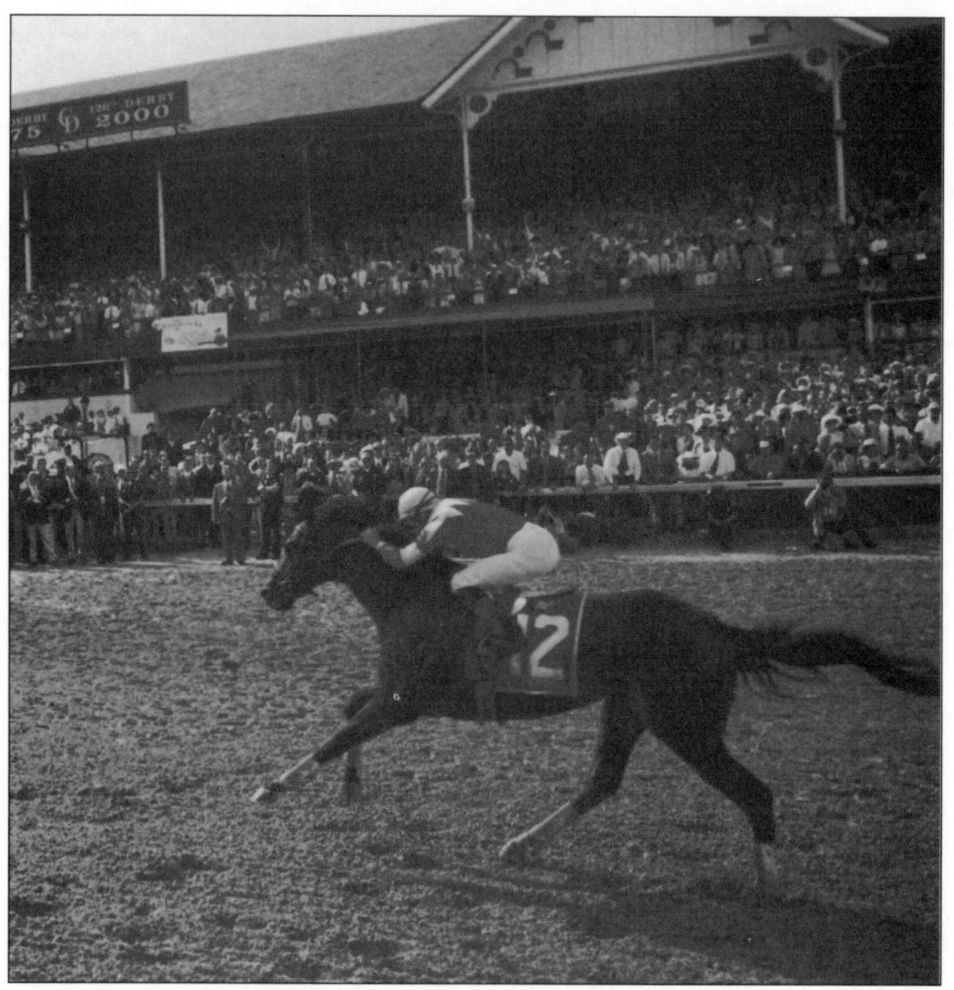

...and won the Kentucky Derby two years later.

Auctions are a reliable source for Derby winners.

question is where's the best place to look for one? The answer, I'm afraid, is just about anywhere there's a guy with a hammer and a bunch of tuxedo-clad gents with a penchant for waving and shouting. If you don't have the time and patience to attend the morass of yearling and two-year-old sales around the country, you can always get a mare, find her a suitable, well-respected beau, and cross your fingers.

Of the past thirty Kentucky Derby winners, twelve were homebreds; four sold at the prestigious

Keeneland July yearling sale in Lexington, Kentucky; three sold at the Keeneland fall yearling sale; three were sold privately; two each were sold at the Fasig-Tipton yearling sale in Saratoga Springs, New York, Fasig-Tipton Kentucky yearling sale, and Ocala Breeders' Sales Company's two-year-old sale in Florida; and one each was sold at the California Thoroughbred Breeders Association's two-year-old sale and Tartan Farm dispersal. One Derby winner, Thunder Gulch, sold as a yearling, then was purchased privately during his two-year-old season. Another, Silver Charm, sold as a weanling and as a yearling, both at Ocala. Spend a Buck was plucked right out of his paddock as a yearling for $12,500. Strike the Gold was purchased privately as a two-year-old from financially troubled Calumet Farm, which had owned and bred eight Kentucky Derby winners.

As I stated earlier, a Kentucky Derby winner can come from anywhere and look like anything — from grand-looking, near-flawless individuals like Fusaichi Pegasus, Secretariat, and Majestic Prince to crooked-legged horses like Canonero II and Real Quiet. The only thing that's worth remembering is that they're all equally beautiful with a blanket of roses draped across their shoulders.

So, how does one begin looking for a Derby horse when there is no standard model as a reference? Most horsemen aren't thinking Kentucky Derby when they look at yearlings. They're usually just looking for well-made, athletic horses with solid pedigrees. Once they've found them, they wait and watch.

Derby horses don't emerge overnight; they slowly take shape like a photograph floating in developer. One minute there is a blank piece of paper, and the next an image begins to appear. Some images become brilliant and sharp and full of action, while others are out of focus and must be discarded or put in the reject pile. A trainer scrutinizes every one of his young horses in the hope that, like the photographer, he'll see that one special award-winning shot develop before his eyes. If it does, the trainer, unlike the photographer, has to hope he doesn't screw it up. And there are a million ways to screw up a horse on the road to the Derby. Remember, only fifteen to twenty horses out of approximately forty thousand Thoroughbreds born in a given year make it to Churchill Downs on the first Saturday in May.

Before you begin having Derby dreams, remember that victory in the Run for the Roses often comes with a price. Of the Derby winners since 1980,

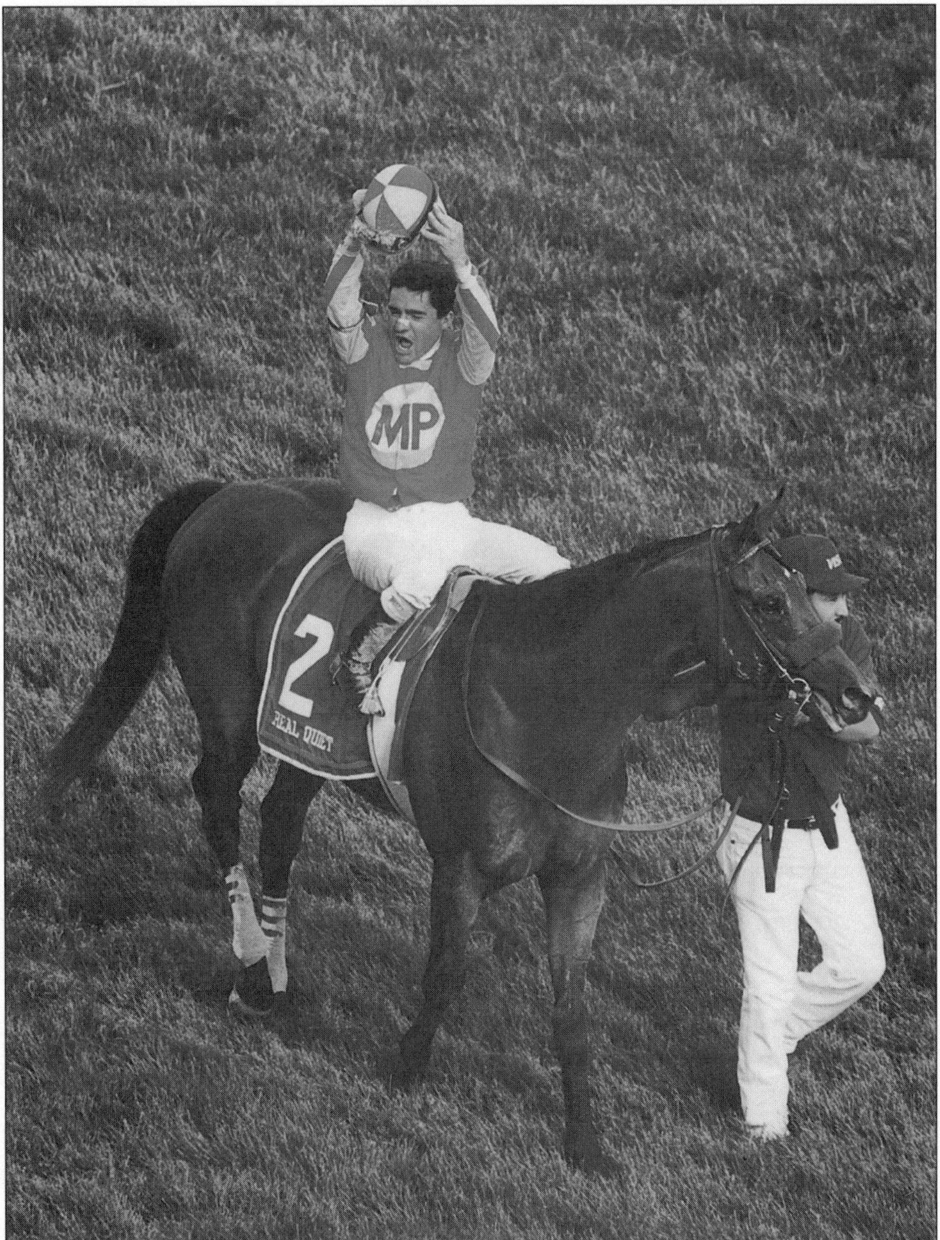

The bargain-priced Real Quiet.

Monarchos, Thunder Gulch, Grindstone, and Charismatic all were injured during their three-year-old campaigns. Grindstone never made it to the Preakness, and Charismatic never made it past the Belmont. Fusaichi Pegasus, Spend a Buck, Sunny's Halo, and Pleasant Colony never made it to their four-year-old campaigns. Swale died mysteriously after the Belmont. Go for Gin never won another stakes. Strike the Gold lost twelve consecutive races following the Derby before winning the Pimlico Special a year later. In 2001 the first six finishers in the Derby all were injured and either retired or were out for the year by late August.

But the Derby is one of the most cherished prizes in all of sport, and the majority of owners and trainers are more than willing to take their chances when immortality is at stake. Just measure the width of the chasm that separates Derby winners from the second-place finishers. Consider Swale and Coax Me Chad, Thunder Gulch and Tejano Run, Ferdinand and Bold Arrangement, Riva Ridge and No Le Hace, Spend a Buck and Stephan's Odyssey, Cannonade and Hudson County, Pleasant Colony and Woodchopper, Genuine Risk and Rumbo, Tim Tam and Lincoln Road. And these are just a few examples from the latter half of the twentieth century. The winners' names still roll off the tongue with ease, while most people have long forgotten the horses that came one horse away from being household names.

The Derby was born of household names like Old Rosebud, Regret, and Exterminator to the fairy tale saga of Black Gold. From those years, between 1914 and 1924, came the foundation of the Kentucky Derby, which was built mainly with words. Words like

Harry Payne Whitney's Regret, the 1915 winner.

those of Regret's owner, Harry Payne Whitney, who said after his filly's victory, "I do not care if she wins another race, or if she never starts in another race. She has won the greatest race in America and I am satisfied." Those words uttered by someone of such prominence single-handedly catapulted the Derby from a struggling event to one of great prestige.

Then there was Irvin S. Cobb, who said, "Until you go to Kentucky and with your own eyes behold a Derby, you ain't never been nowheres and you ain't seen nothin'."

John Steinbeck wrote after his first Derby experience, "This Kentucky Derby, whatever it is — a race, an emotion, a turbulence, an explosion — is one of the most beautiful and violent and satisfying things I have ever experienced. I am glad I have seen and felt it at last."

In 2001 Saudi Arabia's Prince Ahmed Salman, owner of highly favored Point Given, said before the Derby, "One of the great ambitions of my life is to win the Kentucky Derby. I have dreamed of it since I was a child."

The passionate prose that the Derby inspires has allowed it to continue to expand into the very heart and soul of public consciousness. And that is why people will always dream of winning the Kentucky

Derby. They are aware that a victory will allow them to transcend sport and become a part of Americana.

And unlike other great events such as the Super Bowl and the Indianapolis 500, the Kentucky Derby can be won by nearly anyone.

You now know several important factors. Derby winners come in all sizes and shapes; they are more likely to be purchased for bargain-basement prices than for millions; they need not resemble perfect specimens; and they can be purchased just about anywhere Thoroughbreds are sold.

While anyone can own a Derby winner, not anyone can train a Derby winner. And that brings us to our final search. The most important thing for would-be winning owners to remember is not to ask a boy to do a man's job. Of course, one day a young upstart trainer like Cam Gambolati will come up with a running fool like Spend a Buck for a novice owner like Dennis Diaz and have everything fall into place. To this day, no one who was there can explain how Juan Arias and Canonero II were able to pull off perhaps the most mind-boggling victory in Derby history. Here was a $1,200 yearling with obscure bloodlines and crooked knees teaming up with a black trainer who grew up in the slums of Caracas, Venezuela, and who spoke no English, defying all logic and winning America's greatest race. But examples such as this are rarities.

Although a proven, veteran trainer increases the odds of winning, that is by no means a formula for success. Is it a mere coincidence that top-name veteran trainers such as Ron McAnally, Bill Mott, Dick Mandella, Shug

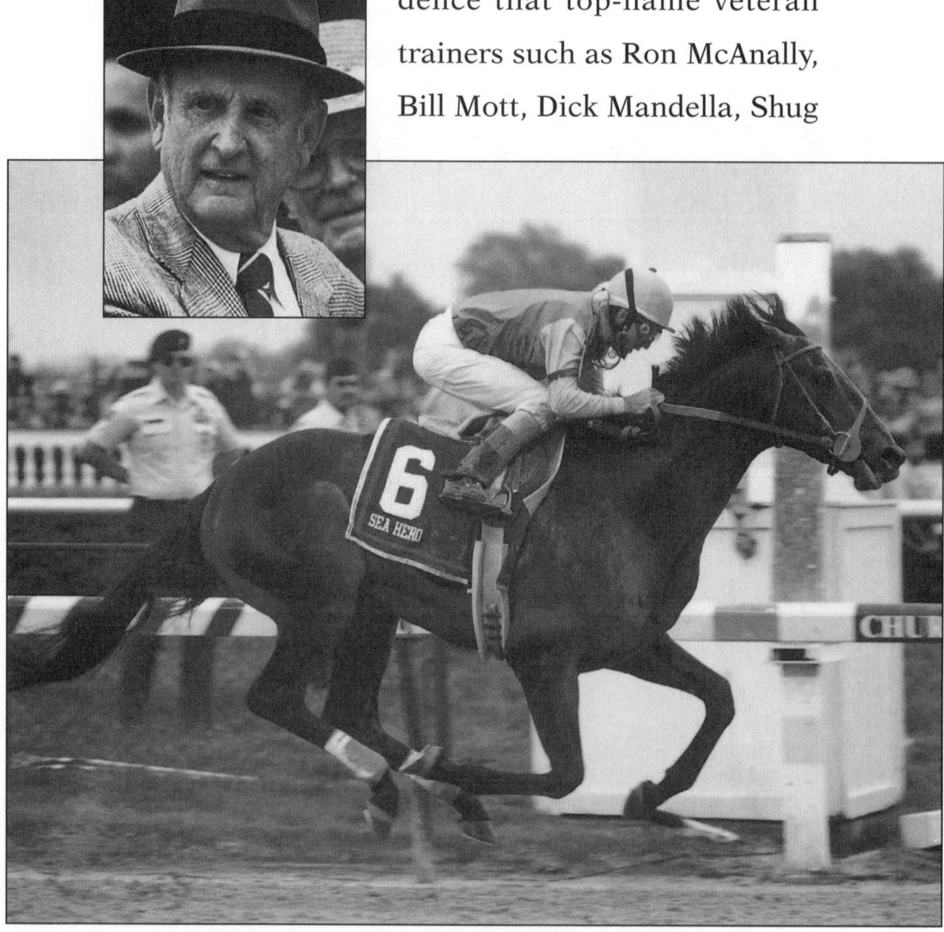

Mack Miller's conservative approach paid off with Sea Hero.

McGaughey, Bobby Frankel, Scotty Schulhofer, Allen Jerkens, and Frank Brothers collectively are zero for thirty-four in the Derby, with thirty-one of their starters finishing out of the money? Other than McAnally with ten starters, none of the others have gotten more than five horses to the starting gate on Derby Day. Heck, Wayne Lukas did that in one year. What's the reason? Are these trainers more conservative in their approach to training? Are they incapable of pushing a horse hard enough to be ready for the Derby ordeal? Are they not getting the right types of horses?

"I wish I knew the secret," said recent Hall of Fame inductee Dick Mandella, who is zero for four in the Derby and has never finished better than fifth. "I could throw out a lot of crap about why I haven't won the Derby, but the truth is I really can't figure it out. When I was in trainer's school, I probably fell asleep when they got to the Derby. Sometimes I sit and wonder what I have to do to even come close. Hell, I'd rob a bank to get to win it."

Neil Drysdale seemed to fit that profile, yet he won the Derby in 2000 with his first-ever starter, Fusaichi Pegasus, who was one of the most lightly trained Derby winners ever. And Mack Miller, trainer of 1993 winner Sea Hero, was as conservative as any of them. The feeling here is that any one of the above-mentioned trainers can win the Derby, given the right horse and the right circumstances.

CHAPTER

The Men from the Boys

Trainers travel a treacherous road to the Derby. The experienced ones can navigate the bumps and potholes, but for those unsuspecting souls traveling on the Derby trail, it is the unforeseen obstacles that usually cause their downfall.

Five days before the 1997 Kentucky Derby, Crypto Star breezed seven furlongs in 1:31, one of the slowest pre-Derby works in quite a while. This came only three days after Ogden Phipps' promising colt Accelerator broke down during a workout. The media converged on Crypto Star's trainer, Wayne Catalano, who also exercised the horse.

"Everything went beautiful," Catalano said in his Cajun drawl. "He handled the track good and finished up good. I could have asked him to go a little faster, but I'm afraid to lay him down on this racetrack. I don't want to be the next one out of the Derby."

Catalano had done a super job with Crypto Star, having captured the Louisiana and Arkansas derbys. But on this day, all signs pointed to Crypto Star as a throw out in the Derby. Catalano knew the colt had

Wayne Catalano shifted to the defense with Crypto Star.

some physical problems (that would surface after the Derby), but he still tried to convince himself, or maybe just the media, that he was happy with the work. By using the word "afraid," and saying he didn't want to be "the next one out of the Derby," he had shifted from offense to defense, and defense does not win the Derby.

Earlier that year, Alan Goldberg, who trained 1990 Breeders' Cup Sprint winner Safely Kept but who had no Derby experience, was hoping to get his promising colt Jules to Churchill Downs. Following a fifth-place finish in a Gulfstream allowance race in which Jules bled slightly, Goldberg said, "I'm a little confused right now." Goodbye Jules.

Confusion and fear are the kiss of death for any trainer, especially one who has never been exposed to all the pitfalls of the Derby trail. Trainers are in the proverbial fish bowl, with all eyes on their every move. At stake is more than a horse race. What they do and how they act can affect the rest of their lives. Ordinary roses die quickly, but the roses presented to the Derby winner live forever. There can be no doubts and certainly no fears. A trainer has to attack the Derby if he is to have any hopes of conquering it. You'd never hear Lukas, Baffert, Zito, Whittingham, or Drysdale ever use the word "confused" or admit they were "afraid" to do something.

A seven-furlong work by Louisiana Derby winner Dixieland Heat before the 1993 Derby really threw the brother team of trainer Gerald Romero and jockey Randy Romero for a loop and had them retreating behind closed doors to try and figure out what had just happened.

Dixieland Heat went out for his morning work

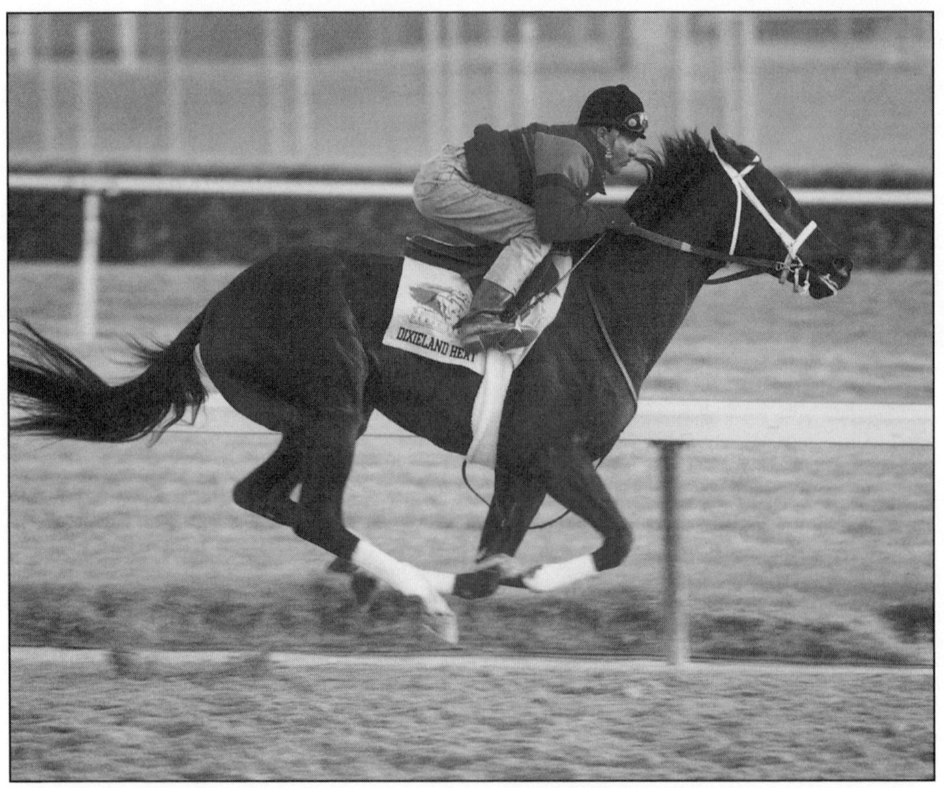

Dixieland Heat began to cool during Derby week...

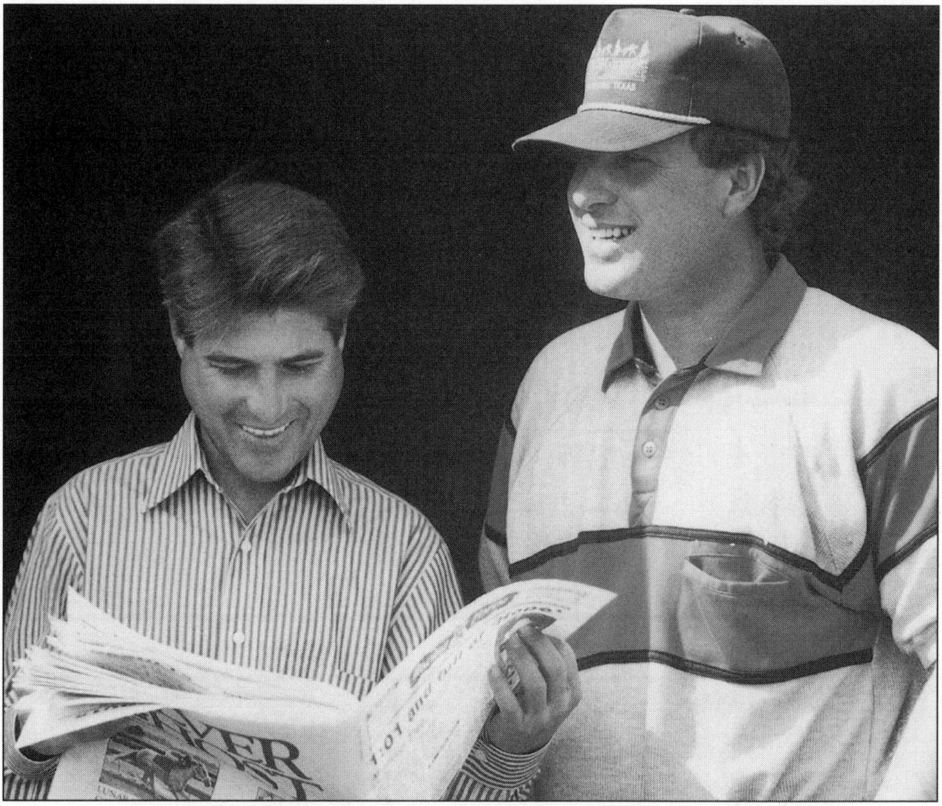

...much to the dismay of Randy and Gerald Romero, who tried to maintain a positive front.

with Randy aboard at 6:30 on the Monday before the Derby. This is officially the red zone; no time or place for mistakes. After a once-around gallop, Dixieland Heat broke off and appeared to be going very easily. Although the colt had his ears pinned back down the stretch, Randy was sitting motionless. After bringing the colt back, Randy walked over to the clocker's stand to get a time of the work. He didn't know what to expect, but he sure wasn't expecting to hear he had waltzed through the seven furlongs in a lethargic 1:35.

Walking back to the barn, Randy was asked if he got the time. "No," he shot back in disgust. After arriving at the barn, he went straight into the office and closed the door. Gerald then went in, and a few minutes later both came out and explained that Randy had felt the track was too slippery and decided to abort the work, giving the colt a two-minute lick instead. We all accepted the explanation even though it was curious why Randy would ask for the time if he

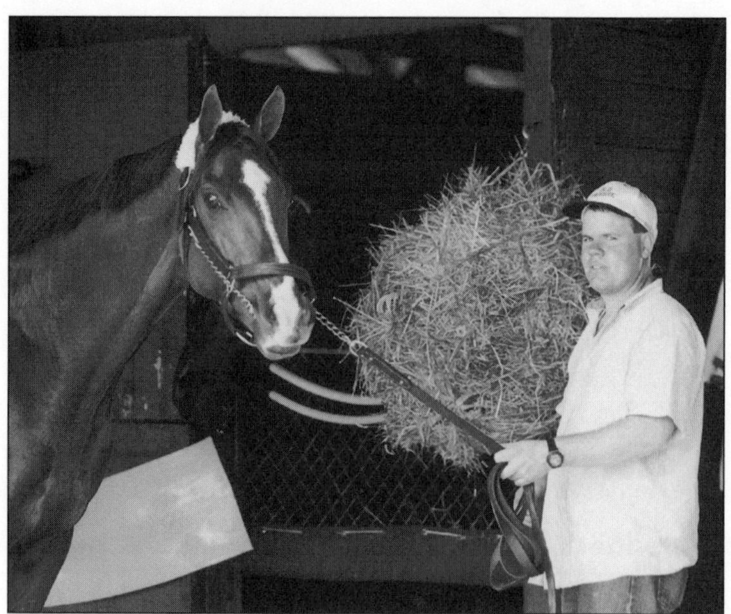

Mike Puype and Old Trieste: youth and speed.

aborted the work. It was decided to work Dixieland Heat the following day, and this time he went six furlongs in a slow, but more respectable, 1:15.

So here was another case of being thrown a monkey wrench at an inopportune time and not knowing how to handle it. Both Randy and Gerald are first-class horsemen, but the Kentucky Derby is a whole different ballgame. In any event, Dixieland Heat was never in the race, finishing twelfth.

In 1998 another Derby novice, Mike Puype, had to confront a situation completely opposite of Catalano's and the Romeros'. Puype had a talented but lightly raced colt named Old Trieste who could fly. A week before the Derby, Puype watched in shock as Old Trieste worked six furlongs in a scorching 1:09 flat, the fastest pre-Derby work anyone had ever seen or even heard of. As he departed the box area, he said, "I don't know whether to smile or throw up."

When a trainer doesn't know if a final Derby work is good or bad, he's in serious trouble. In Puype's defense, he was encountering something totally unforeseen, and he simply did not have the experience to deal with it. Old Trieste, true to form, set the early pace, sizzling six furlongs in a brisk 1:10 3/5 before fading to tenth.

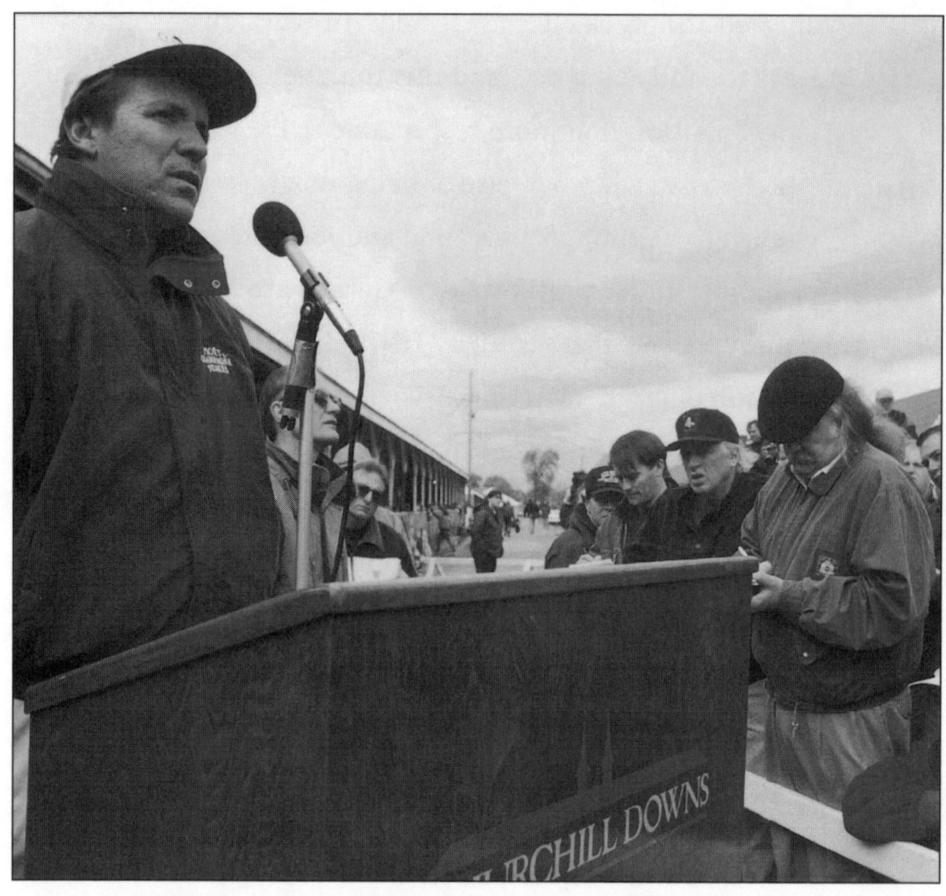

Jim Ryerson gave daily briefings about Unbridled's Song.

I've seen many young, inexperienced trainers become unraveled on the road to Louisville, and some after arriving at Churchill Downs. It has nothing to do with their ability as trainers. It's just that the Kentucky Derby has a way of setting traps along the way, and unsuspecting, inexperienced trainers have less chance of avoiding them or dealing with them once they've fallen in. Two such trainers were Jim Ryerson and Randy Winick, both of whom came to Kentucky with extraordinarily talented horses. But when Unbridled's Song, the strong early Derby favorite in 1996, came out of the Wood Memorial with a foot problem, it created a circus atmosphere around Ryerson's barn, something he was not prepared to deal with. The young trainer tried to handle it, but it got out of control and created bad feelings between him and owner Ernie Paragallo.

Each day Churchill Downs officials had to set up a podium outside Ryerson's barn, where he would give a 10 a.m. press conference in front of a huddled mass of frozen reporters and TV and radio people. Ryerson had been to the Derby once before with longshot Meadow Flight, but in training the hot favorite, this kind of distraction is something very few trainers are equipped to handle.

It was bad enough that Ryerson had to deal with the quarter crack and a Z-bar shoe to protect it, but early in Derby Week the foot flared up, and veterinarians were called in to work frantically into the late afternoon. It eventually was decided to replace the Z-bar shoe with a more cumbersome egg-bar shoe, named, simply, for its egg shape. That night, fellow scribe Ed

Fountaine and I were supposed to take Ryerson and Buzz Chace, Paragallo's bloodstock agent and adviser, out to dinner at Pat's Steak House. We had no idea what had happened, but the silence at dinner was so thick you could have cut it with one of Pat's steak knives. Buzz stared out the window the entire night, chain-smoking without saying a word.

Unbridled's Song, despite running in two egg-bar shoes, turned in an incredible performance, opening up a clear lead in 1:35 flat before tiring to finish fifth. He still was beaten less than four lengths, and a neck and a nose for third. Paragallo still fumes about the colt's going into battle wearing the two bar shoes. Would he have won or finished closer wearing a patch instead, something several blacksmiths felt he should have been wearing? Would a more experienced trainer have done things differently or kept in closer communication with the owner? Ryerson obviously was advised by reputable people, and he went along with it. As for the "what might have beens," you can throw them in the manure pile.

The day after the Derby, in front of Ryerson's barn, the podium still stood. Now merely a relic of Derby 122, it served only as a faint reminder of the previous week's turmoil. Curled up inside was Ryerson's black cat Lucky. Talk about one picture being worth a thousand words. Ryerson and Paragallo eventually parted company and Unbridled's Song ended up in the barn of Nick Zito for the colt's abbreviated four-year-old season.

Sharing the barn with Ryerson that year was another trainer new to the Derby scene, Bob Baffert. Baffert observed with interest all the chaos on the other end of the barn and saw firsthand what can happen when things fall apart before the Derby. After Unbridled's Song's problems were compounded when he drew post twenty, the fun-loving Baffert just shook his head and said, "How can any horse in my barn have such bad karma?" Even though Baffert's Cavonnier suffered a heart-breaking nose defeat in the Derby that year, the trainer learned from the experience and has since become one of the most dominant forces in Triple Crown history.

As for Randy Winick's colt Brocco, the Breeders' Cup Juvenile winner had just won the 1994 Santa Anita Derby, establishing himself as one of the main Kentucky Derby contenders, along with the brilliant Holy Bull. But when Brocco was placed on the vet's list by the Santa Anita stewards after supposedly coming out of the race "very, very slightly off in one

Captain Bodgit (outside) nearly did it in 1997, a testament to trainer Gary Capuano's skill.

of his front legs," Winick lost his cool. "This is a joke," he said disgustedly. "This is going to cause me nothing but heartache and aggravation. The whole incident has been a nightmare. I haven't been able to enjoy anything."

Although Winick had every right to be upset, who knows just how much his bad vibes rubbed off on Brocco, who had vets hounding him and taking his blood when he should have been on a strict training regimen with no distractions? Whatever the reasons, Brocco wound up finishing fourth in the slop, and Winick eventually disappeared into obscurity.

Of course, there are exceptions to every rule, and one exception to this one may be Gary Capuano, the young Maryland-based trainer who handled Captain Bodgit like a seasoned pro in 1997. The Captain, who had won the Laurel Futurity the year before, was purchased early in 1997 by Team Valor despite an old tendon injury that blew the colt's ankle up to the size of a softball. It would become quite a conversation piece and ammunition for the skeptics in the weeks leading up to the Derby. Instead of switching to a more experienced trainer, Team Valor decided to keep the colt with Capuano, who had never won a stakes outside of Maryland and was based at the Bowie training center.

After winning the Florida Derby, Captain Bodgit was supposed to run in the Blue Grass Stakes, but his nomination turned up missing, which precipitated a last-minute switch to the Wood Memorial, which the Captain won anyway in the slop. Sent off as the favorite in the Derby, he was beaten a head by Silver Charm before losing another photo finish in the Preakness, then breaking down while training for the Belmont. Capuano, despite his inexperience and having to deal with the colt's ankle and an unexpected detour in the road, handled everything like a consummate professional, including the two heartbreaking defeats and the career-ending injury. For his training of Captain Bodgit, Capuano earned the admiration and respect of Baffert, who complimented him after the Derby on the exceptional job he had done.

So, did Capuano do an exceptional job or was Captain Bodgit such an exceptional horse he could have been trained by anyone? Could that head margin have been reversed by a trainer with more experience? That's all purely conjecture. The fact is, in any given year, even a Gary Capuano or a Cam Gambolati (1985 Derby winner Spend a Buck) is dangerous with the right horse.

But that is the exception, and as wide a gap as there is between the inexperienced trainers and the veterans, there's an equally wide gap between veteran Hall of Fame trainers who have tried unsuccessfully for years to win the Derby and those who have had great success. Which brings us to Lukas, Baffert, and Zito.

CHAPTER

Derby Dynamos

I eat, sleep, drink, and bleed the Derby and the Triple Crown."

So said Nick Zito. D. Wayne Lukas and Bob Baffert could make the same statement. Although none have won the Derby in the last two years, they dominated the Run for the Roses in the nineties, winning in 1991, '94, '95, '96, '97, '98, and '99. Lukas also was victorious in 1988. Despite the fact that all three trainers have virtually nothing in common, they all share one thing: an almost-obsessive desire to smell the roses on the first Saturday in May.

This chapter is devoted to their never-ending quest and ultimate success. Lukas began the juggernaut in 1988 with the filly Winning Colors. Zito won in 1991 with Strike the Gold and in 1994 with Go for Gin. Then it was Lukas' turn again, as he captured the 1995 and '96 runnings with Thunder Gulch and

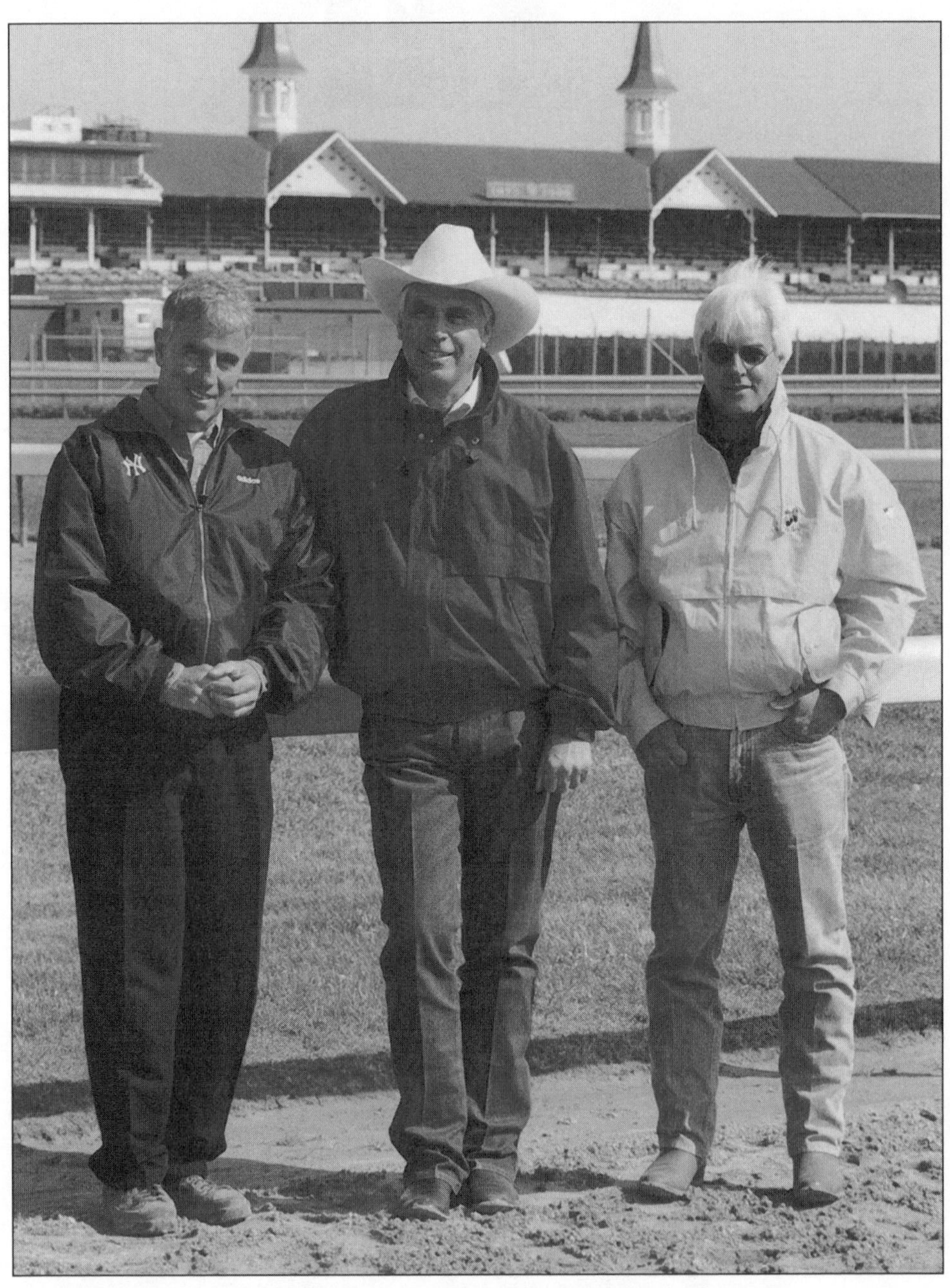

Derby masters Nick Zito, Wayne Lukas, and Bob Baffert.

Grindstone, respectively. The dynamic duo became the triumphant trio when Bob Baffert exploded on the scene, winning in 1997 with Silver Charm and '98 with Real Quiet. He had telegraphed his intentions in 1996, getting beaten a nose with the California-bred gelding Cavonnier. Lukas then ended the decade in rousing fashion, finishing first and third in 1999 with Charismatic and Cat Thief.

While Zito and Baffert were able to win the Derby in their second attempt, it took Lukas seven unsuccessful years and twelve starters before he finally made it to the winner's circle with Winning Colors in 1988.

"It was a learning process," Lukas said. "I tried it with different types of horses, and I learned from each one. The first time I ran a horse in a classic, I won the Preakness with Codex. The next year I finished third in the Derby with Partez, who was an allowance horse. I said to myself, 'Hell, this is no big deal; I'll win one of these soon enough.' But what I didn't know at the time was that you have to respect the Derby and realize how tough it is."

What's amazing is that in his three Derby victories after Winning Colors, Lukas also finished third each time. In 1995 and '96, he managed to get an incredible eight horses to the starting gate. And in one of the great feats in racing history, he captured six consecutive Triple Crown races, starting with the 1994 Preakness and ending with the 1996 Kentucky Derby. After losing the Preakness that year (to Zito's Louis Quatorze), he came right back to win the Belmont.

Lukas has performed wonders in the Derby, winning with a filly, a lightly raced colt with a bum knee (Grindstone), a 25-1 shot who was considered the third string of his three Derby entries (Thunder Gulch), and a former claimer (Charismatic) who was making his third start in four weeks and ridden by his fifth jockey in his last six races. There isn't much Lukas hasn't seen. From the first of the year, he is honed in on the first Saturday in May. "He will become more intense as the Derby gets closer," his wife, Laura, said. "But he never loses focus of his game plan."

Lukas continued to pile up Triple Crown scores in 1999 with Charismatic, but in 2000 he finished twelfth, fifteenth, and seventeenth in the Derby, and in 2001, he failed to have a starter for the first time in twenty years. He still managed to sneak in another Triple Crown victory, upsetting the 2000 Belmont with Commendable.

One thing Lukas, Baffert, and Zito will agree on is that the Derby can be a humbling experience, no matter who you are. As quickly as it can catapult you to the ultimate heights, that's how quickly it can bring you crashing down. Baffert has sent six powerful entries to the Derby since his victory with Real Quiet in 1998, but finished out of the money with five of them. Zito has now gone seven years without winning, and all nine of his starters during that time finished out of the money.

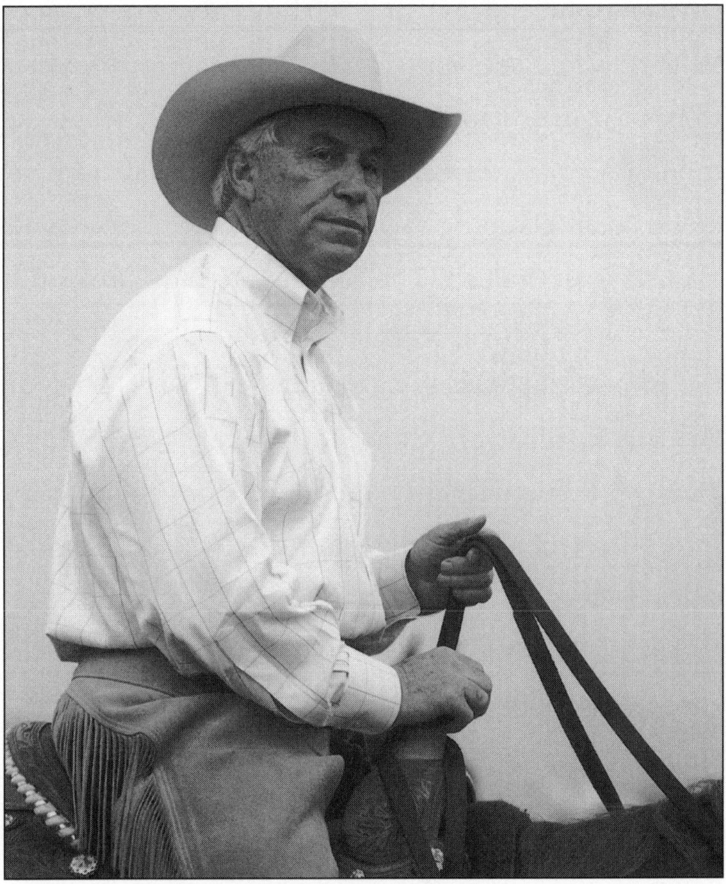

Lukas practically owned the Triple Crown races in the nineties.

But even when they don't win the Derby, they still usually manage to get there with top-class horses such as Point Given, Congaree, General Challenge, Indian Charlie, Captain Steve, Cavonnier (Baffert); Louis Quatorze, Halory Hunter, Stephen Got Even, A P Valentine (Zito); and Tabasco Cat, Timber Country, Editor's Note, Tank's Prospect, and High Yield (Lukas).

After planning his pre-Derby itinerary for A P Valentine in 2001, Zito saw his plans crumble when the colt's shins kept flaring up. With his schedule in total disarray, Zito was forced to run A P Valentine in an optional claiming race (for allowance horses and claimers) at Hialeah. The son of A.P. Indy broke the track record but came back and ran a dismal race in the Blue Grass Stakes. Zito had no answers. Most of the colt's followers dumped him like yesterday's garbage. Some trainers might have stuck their heads in a hole and simply quit, but Zito knew his horse and believed in him, and he pushed on. A P Valentine had a nightmare trip in the Derby, having to take up sharply twice on the far turn while making his run. He still managed to close from fourteenth at the head of the stretch to finish a respectable seventh. Zito and many others were positive he would have finished in the money with a clean trip. So Zito pushed on. A P

Valentine wound up finishing second in the Preakness and Belmont to Point Given, re-establishing himself as one of the best of his generation.

The point of this is to show what an experienced Derby trainer can accomplish when everything goes against him. Zito was confronted with obstacles that would have stopped most trainers, but he knew how to get around them and managed to come away with a pair of second-place finishes with a horse just about everyone had given up for dead.

Success on this high a scale, however, does bring with it microscopic scrutiny that not only magnifies strengths, but reveals weaknesses as well. Lukas, Baffert, and Zito all have volatile personalities that will erupt if probed and pricked enough times. Success in racing does not thicken the skin, and one must tread carefully around high-profile figures who are easily bruised. A case in point is this scene from from the morning after Grindstone's victory in 1996:

It was 4:00 a.m. the day after the Derby, and the blue and amber lights of the Twin Spires seemed to shine down directly onto Barn 45. All was black except for the tons of discarded programs, tickets, and other trash that had piled up like snowdrifts in the night. Wayne Lukas' two Australian shepherds,

Shine and Fallon, were racing in and out of the barn, enjoying the crisp morning air. Their master had not yet arrived, having been detained at his favorite Louisville doughnut shop by well-wishers.

Inside the barn, the grooms began stirring, filtering out of their tack rooms. Grindstone peered out his stall, then took a few nibbles from his hay rack. Lukas' four other Derby starters, Editor's Note, Victory Speech, Prince of Thieves, and Honour and Glory, all appeared none the worse for wear.

Lukas arrived at 4:15 and explained why he was "late." He then took the opportunity to reflect on the mixed emotions he was feeling. On one hand, this was one of his most satisfying and emotional victories. It meant a great deal to him to have won the Derby for William T. Young, who had been Lukas' most loyal supporter during the trainer's two-and-a-half-year slump, during which time the trainer did not win a single grade I stakes.

On the other hand, he still was hurt and angry over a story that appeared in the *Louisville Courier-Journal* that made him look more like an egotistical marketing genius than a horseman. The story discussed the trainer's lending of his name to a clothing line and to a local car dealership. If there is one thing in which

Lukas takes pride, it's his ability as a horseman, and to have several of his fellow trainers say otherwise in print upset him. He even confronted Bob Baffert, one of those quoted, in the President's Room on Derby Day, as Baffert was celebrating his victory with Criollito in the Churchill Downs Handicap.

Lukas couldn't hold back his feelings any longer, and he spilled his guts out to me. I used his quotes verbatim in my lead story on the front page of the *Daily Racing Form*. They read as follows: "What did I ever do to deserve this? I really had to bite my tongue at the

Lukas won the '96 Derby for loyal supporter W.T. Young.

press conference in respect to Mr. Young. I stand out here for four or five hours a day and try to do my job, and they've got me as some Barnum & Bailey guy that doesn't know a thing about a horse. I can't be somebody I'm not. Am I supposed to come here and wear different type of clothes or change my whole makeup? I'm not supposed to be competent? I'm not supposed to be a good speaker? If a guy wants to put my name on a label of clothing, I should say no because I'm a horse trainer? The quotes from the other trainers were very damaging and I'm having trouble handling that. I'm proud of my staff and I'm proud of what we've done. That's what we are; deal with it."

I mention this incident to show what life at the top can be like. Baffert, who claims his quotes in the article were taken out of context, would be on the receiving end five years later after he too reached the pinnacle of his profession. The heat from the spotlight can be very hot, and the once-amiable Baffert became more cynical toward the media, banning several reporters from his barn after his personal life went public. It took only three years for the love affair between Baffert, a one-time Quarter Horse trainer from Arizona, and the media to sour. One year, Zito, who alleged he was hounded to distraction by a female reporter, had to answer charges that he struck the reporter across the mouth with his rolled up program. The charges against the New York City native were dismissed.

But the three trainers didn't allow these distractions to interfere with their mission. Each continued to zero in on the Triple Crown and the Breeders' Cup like a fighter pilot with an enemy plane in his sights. That is a major reason for their success. And that's what makes them so dangerous.

But the ability of Zito, Baffert, and Lukas to win the Derby and send live horses there year after year is about all they have in common. Each has completely different training styles, yet all manage to attain the same objective.

Lukas rides a pony in the morning. Zito and Baffert don't. Zito washes down his horses himself after training. Lukas and Baffert don't. Baffert uses a two-way radio to keep in constant contact with his exercise riders. Lukas and Zito don't. Lukas and Baffert wear cowboy boots and jeans. Zito wears work shoes and trousers. Zito is a wine connoisseur and rarely orders off a menu; Baffert likes Diet Coke and fast food, as well as a fun night out at a good restaurant; Lukas is content with a hamburger and a glass of milk from room service.

Although they might work their horses differently Derby week, all three have their horses fit and ready for the big day. Baffert's two Derby winners, Silver Charm and Real Quiet, each had three workouts at Churchill Downs prior to the Derby, and of the six works, five were bullet moves, or the fastest work on the tab. The only one that wasn't was Real Quiet's six-

Baffert's initial lovefest with the media soured.

furlong work in 1:12 2/5, and that was second only to Baffert's other Derby starter Indian Charlie, who worked out before Real Quiet when the track was freshly harrowed and playing faster.

Lukas' four Derby winners, on the other hand, did not have a single bullet work among them, although they usually were solid works — in the 1:13 to 1:14 range for six furlongs, and 1:00 to 1:01 for five furlongs. Zito, however, worked Go for Gin five furlongs in a slow 1:04 3/5 and six furlongs in 1:15. Strike the Gold breezed five furlongs in a pedestrian 1:05 and a half-mile in :51 2/5, but did throw in a bullet five-furlong work in 1:00 flat in between.

When Lukas gave Thunder Gulch his final work for the Derby, he wasn't expecting the mini-drama that would take place down the stretch. Lukas decided to remove Thunder Gulch's blinkers and work him in company with a four-year-old filly named Neeran. When jockey Donna Barton, aboard Thunder Gulch, asked him to put the filly away in the stretch, the colt had other ideas. Not only did he refuse to pass her, he kept leaning in on her, despite Barton's snapping the whip at him several times with her left hand. At the wire, Neeran finished a neck ahead of Thunder Gulch, who, unbeknownst to anyone at the time was providing a look into the future at his affection for the ladies and his remarkable success in the breeding shed.

"I should have known better than to take the blinkers off and work him with a filly," Lukas said after the work. "I took them off because I thought he might be too aggressive and I didn't want him to overdo it. With the blinkers, he would have gone right by that filly." Just the way he went right by everyone else a week later in the Derby.

So, it's apparent there is no formula on how to work a horse before the Derby, as long as trainers know their horse and what it needs. You rarely, if ever, see a horse work a mile for the Derby. Most trainers, especially the younger ones, tend to play it safe and not ask too much of their horse in the morning.

But there was one trainer who did believe in working his Derby horses a mile. His name was Charlie Whittingham, and he was never one to follow a crowd. After arriving at Churchill in 1986, Whittingham worked Ferdinand five furlongs in a sizzling :58 3/5, followed by a mile in 1:38 4/5 and seven furlongs in 1:24 3/5. Ferdinand won comfortably, paying $37.40. In 1989 Whittingham followed almost the exact same pattern with Sunday Silence, working the son of Halo a blistering half in :46 3/5, a mile in 1:39

3/5 in the slop, then seven furlongs in 1:28. Sunday Silence won comfortably, upsetting heavy favorite Easy Goer. In 1994 Whittingham was trying to buck history with the lightly raced Strodes Creek, who came into the race with only four career starts under

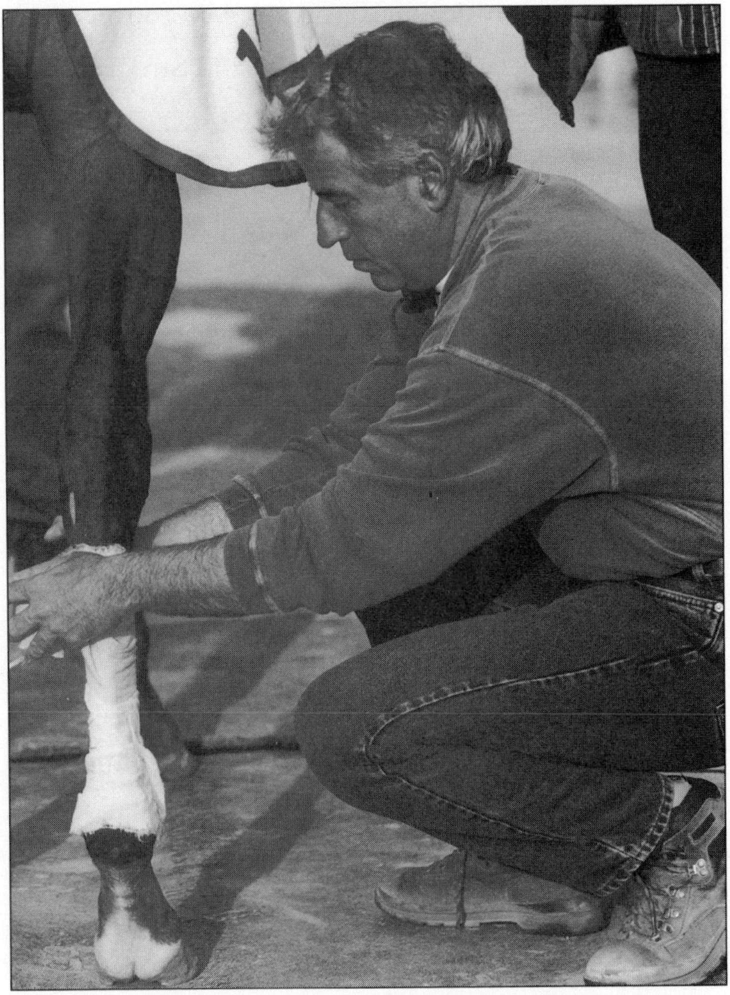

Zito is more of a hands-on trainer than Lukas or Baffert.

his belt. Whittingham didn't think the towering son of Halo needed fast works, nor was the colt comfortable with them, being more of a lazy horse in the morning. Whittingham gave him a slow five-furlong breeze in 1:03 4/5, but did come right back five days later with a stiffer mile work in 1:42 4/5, followed by another five-furlong breeze in 1:02 2/5. Strodes Creek finished a fast-closing second to Go for Gin in the slop at odds of almost 8-1.

Despite Whittingham's success working his Derby horses a mile, no other Derby-winning trainer has worked his horse that far since David Cross did it in 1983 with Sunny's Halo, who needed a long work, having had only two starts that year. The reason it's not done, obviously, is that most trainers race their horse within three weeks of the Derby. Whittingham brought all three colts to Churchill immediately following the Santa Anita Derby, giving him an extra week. No one could train a horse up to a race better than the Bald Eagle, and he played to his strength. But remember, there was only one Charlie Whittingham, which is why no one has attempted to copy his unique training methods. The philosophy now is, "Don't screw it up." No matter how cocky a young trainer may seem, deep down he knows his limitations and plays it safe. That is why experienced trainers who are confident enough in their own ability to work a horse fast or slow, short or long, win the Derby every year.

Some young trainers with their heads on straight, like Todd Pletcher, will take home the roses quicker than others. The no-nonsense Pletcher, who learned under Lukas, finished fourth, third, and second in 2000 and 2001, and there no doubt is a Derby with his name on it. Another Lukas disciple who is beginning to make waves on the classic trail is Dallas Stewart. He's more cocky than Pletcher and much more prone to braggadocio when it comes to his horses, but he's also learned his lessons well from the master and doesn't get rattled when things don't go his way.

The bottom line is that certain trainers have shown they have a knack for getting a horse to the Derby and bringing out the best in him (or her) on that one given day. LeRoy Jolley certainly did from 1975 to 1980, during which time he saddled two winners (Foolish Pleasure in 1975 and Genuine Risk in 1980) and two second-place finishers (Honest Pleasure in '76 and General Assembly in '79).

Even with Lukas, Baffert, and Zito, you're dealing with a double-edged sword. They have proven they know how to get a horse to the Derby and what it takes to win it, but they also train a good number of talented youngsters that don't make it to the Derby.

Among them were the brilliant stakes-winning two-year-olds Exploit, Flame Thower, Boston Harbor, Forest Camp, Souvenir Copy, Hennessy, Grand Slam, Greenwood Lake, The Groom Is Red, Acceptable, Salt Lake, Deposit Ticket, and Tactical Cat, to name a few.

But they still are the three you want to turn to. Unlike the other trainers, they have Derby on their mind from the time they step into the sales pavilions to buy yearlings. Although they have the clients and the resources to stock up on young, promising Derby-type colts to go along with a number of well-bred homebreds, the majority of their Derby winners were inexpensive yearlings. They simply have an uncanny ability to pick out young horses.

Lukas generally likes a little bigger, stronger horse with a good girth and strong quarters, but the animal has to have the conformation to go with it. He paid $575,000 for Winning Colors, an Amazon of a filly who towered over her victims in the 1988 Derby. "If we're going to go over $250,000, we feel they have to have classic conformation and pedigree," Lukas said. "If we go lower than that, we'll compromise. We also like to have good two-year-olds, because two-year-old

Baffert and Silver Charm, one of his "ham sandwiches."

racing is so attractive, but when we're up around the $500,000 and $600,000 range, they must have the pedigree to go a mile and a quarter and the conformation that is conducive to longer distances. Muscle is beautiful, but if they have to drag it around too much it's not good. That's why you need balance and efficiency of movement. That's what wins the Derby; the ability to get over the ground with little effort."

Zito seems to like his horses more on the smaller side, like Go for Gin (a $150,000 yearling), not packing too much weight. But like Lukas, Zito considers balance very important. Baffert will buy anything, from skinny, crooked-legged horses like Real Quiet ($17,000 yearling) to big, muscular horses like Silver Charm ($80,000 two-year-old), as long as he can see the potential that they'll one day develop into the kind of balanced, athletic horse he likes. He used to refer to his horses as ham sandwiches, until the bigger bucks came around and he began buying more expensive yearlings. He also discovered a gold mine in the brothers J.B. and Kevin McKathan, who do most of the dirty work, looking at thousands of yearlings a year, then narrowing down the list for Baffert to make the final choices.

Zito is a blue-collar trainer with a rich man's taste, but he never had the funds or the clientele to compete with Lukas. Everything he accomplished he did with horses in the $50,000 to $150,000 range, much as Baffert used to do. At the 1994 Keeneland July yearling sale, for example, Zito fell in love with a Storm

Zito and Go for Gin, who cost $150,000.

Cat colt and showed me the high rating and comment he had marked down in his catalogue. But the $500,000 price the colt sold for was out of his and main client William Condren's league. He lost the horse to Lukas. Named Hennessy, the colt would go on to win the Hopeful, Sapling, and Hollywood Juvenile Championship before getting beat a neck by Unbridled's Song in the Breeders' Cup Juvenile. It was frustrating for Zito during those years, but he now has deeper pockets with Rick Pitino, Tracy Farmer, Mary Lou Whitney, and several others.

No one will deny that the road to Louisville can be a perilous one, which makes the big three's accomplishments even more remarkable. In 1997 Baffert had Silver Charm heading for the Derby, but he also had another exciting prospect named Inexcessivelygood, whom he ran in the $600,000 Jim Beam Stakes at Turfway Park. While battling down the stretch, Inexcessivelygood broke his leg and fell to the ground. He was euthanized on the track. "He was getting rubber-legged, but he kept digging in trying to battle back, and it cost him his life," a shaken Baffert said later that day. But it's something a trainer has to put behind him, and Baffert pushed ahead with Silver Charm. In the span of a month, Baffert would experience the exultation of winning the Derby and the pain of losing a courageous, talented horse. "That's the price you pay for the Kentucky Derby," he said.

Despite the ones who never made it, when all is said and done, Lukas, Baffert, and Zito are the three guys who know how to pick 'em out, weed 'em out, and send 'em out loaded for bear on the first Saturday in May.

CHAPTER

The Edge

No matter how successful you are in racing, or in anything for that matter, you never stop looking for an edge over your competitors.

One of the challenges of the Derby is that young three-year-olds are going a mile and a quarter for the first time, and attempting this arduous task in a circus-like atmosphere can rattle the calmest of nerves. Because of these unpredictable factors, the Derby is conducted on a much more level playing field than other races, and you never know what single little advantage is going to mean the difference between winning and losing.

In 1997 noted veterinarian Alex Harthill tried to find that edge for his patient Captain Bodgit, so he convinced Barry Irwin, president of Team Valor, to let him install an unusual-looking bungalow-like screen door to ensure security and privacy. Referred to as

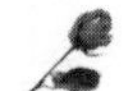

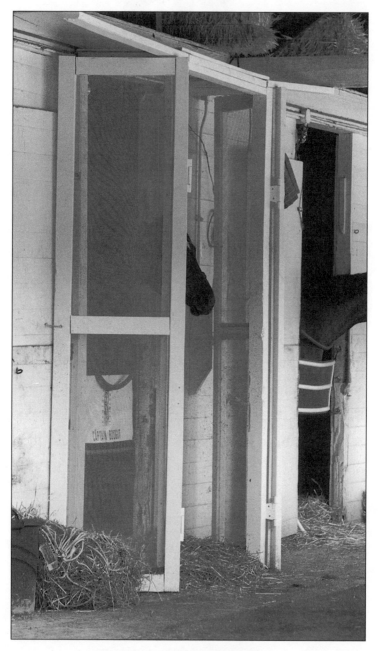

Captain Bodgit's privacy door.

"the contraption" by Irwin, it was first conceived by legendary trainer Ben Jones, who was a master at taking advantage of every edge he could find. No one knew how easy it was to sabotage a horse's chances more than Jones and his son Jimmy. Back in the old days, whenever they were facing a horse they knew was going to be tough to beat, they'd sneak into the horse's stall the night before the race while the help was sleeping or out drinking. They'd then take turns getting on the horse and riding him around so he wouldn't get any rest. The following day, the horse, with no rest and packing all that weight the night before, would be worn out by post time. Years later, when the Jones Boys ruled the sport, Ben never forgot how easy it was to get to a horse, and he devised the screen door.

In 1992 jockey Pat Day felt that adding a shadow roll to Lil E. Tee's equipment might help the colt. Day told trainer Lynn Whiting he thought Lil E. Tee was carrying his head too high in his races. Whiting added the shadow roll for Lil E. Tee's final work before the Derby, and Day said afterward he definitely could feel a difference in the colt. Now, no one is going to say the addition of a shadow roll won the Derby for Lil E. Tee, but it's also hard to say for sure it didn't give him just the little edge he needed to turn in the race of his life.

I've never seen a trainer look for an edge more than Neil Drysdale — regardless of the race. One of the best examples of Drysdale's inspired thinking was his decision to van A.P. Indy to Aqueduct from Belmont Park for the colt's final work prior to the 1992 Belmont Stakes. A torrential downpour during the night had turned the Belmont track into a quagmire, and most trainers either canceled their works or went

Lil E. Tee's shadow roll, suggested by Pat Day, certainly didn't hurt.

into them with great apprehension. Drysdale, however, had an inspiration. On the slight chance it hadn't rained as hard or even at all at Aqueduct, which is only about ten miles away, Drysdale hopped in his car at the crack of dawn and headed down the Belt Parkway to see what the track looked like. Sure enough, Aqueduct was bone dry. Drysdale arranged to van A.P. Indy to the Big A, and the colt turned in a big six-furlong work over a fast track. A week later, he captured the Belmont Stakes.

In 2000 Drysdale had the task of getting the immensely talented, but high-spirited and stubborn, Fusaichi Pegasus to the Derby in top shape, physically and mentally. Drysdale decided it was in the colt's best interests to train him very lightly. The days went by, and all Fusaichi did was jog and gallop. No one had seen anything like it, especially for a Derby favorite. Although Drysdale does nothing by the book, the media still kept asking him when Fusaichi Pegasus was going to work. All they got back were answers like, "Who knows, maybe I won't work him at all," or "He'll ring me up in the middle of the night and tell me when he's ready to work." Fusaichi eventually did work six days before the race, breezing six furlongs in 1:14 3/5.

A spirited Fusaichi Pegasus made Derby preparations a challenge for Neil Drysdale.

Fusaichi's antics in the mornings made things even more interesting. Sent out each day under the cover of darkness, the big colt reared walking back from his gallop one morning, then went down on his hindquarters and rolled over, unseating his rider. It took an alert Drysdale to rush onto the track and grab hold of the lead shank just as the horse was getting back up on his feet.

But if there was one thing that everyone could count on, it was Fusaichi's romp in the sand pen near the Longfield Avenue fence every morning after training. No one else used the pen, which actually belonged to Lukas and was kept under lock and key. But Drysdale got permission to use it, and every morning he'd pick up the key from Lukas' barn and let Fusaichi roll around and kick up a storm. The colt was able to douse a lot of his fire in the sand pen, which had to have helped settle him for the chaotic atmosphere of the Derby. Fusaichi was a perfect gentleman from the time he left the barn and won the Derby under a hand ride.

The following year, a trainer who was stabled right near the pen complained that Lukas' horses were disrupting his horses. He parked his car in front of the

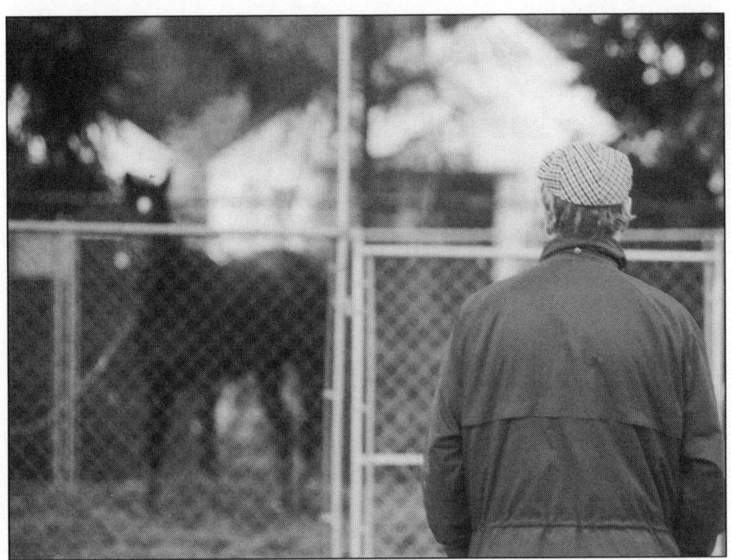

A sand pen helped take the edge off.

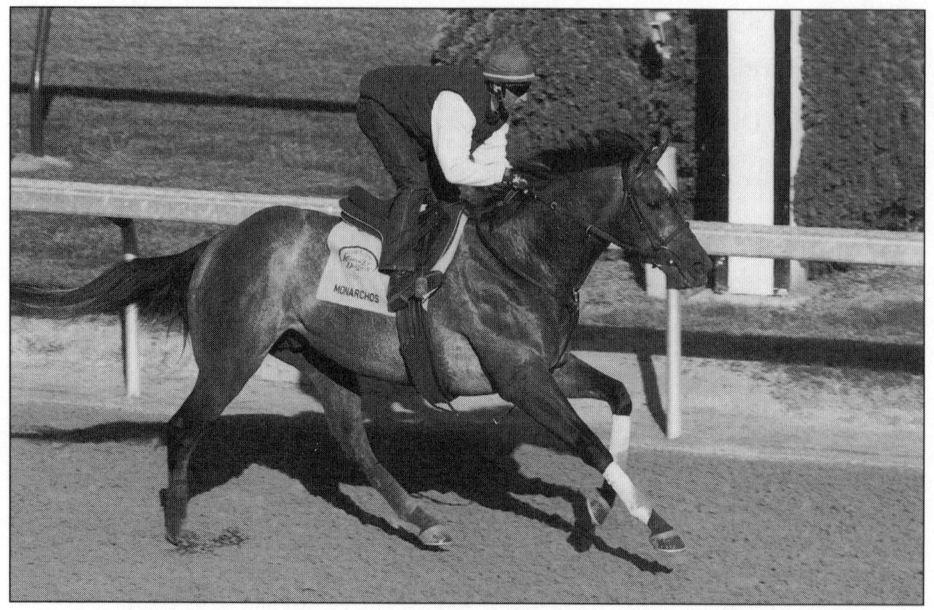

Monarchos had only one serious work before the Derby.

gate of the pen so no one could get in. Lukas in turn disassembled the pen and rebuilt it around the trainer's car, then locked the gate.

Mack Miller, another conservative trainer, needed any kind of an edge just to get Sea Hero to the Derby in 1993. The son of Polish Navy was a nervous, hyper colt and he "melted" in the Florida heat that year, as Miller put it. Having all but run himself out of the Derby picture, Sea Hero needed a shot in the arm, and he needed it fast. Miller, instead of sending him to Keeneland as he normally would have done, shipped Sea Hero to his winter base in Aiken, South Carolina, not where you'd expect to find a Derby horse in April. There, the colt thrived in the cool mornings and nights and did a complete turnaround. After Miller watched him blossom mentally and physically and become competitive once again, he decided to return the colt to the Derby trail, sending him to Keeneland about a week before the Blue Grass Stakes. Sea Hero became involved in a shoving match in the stretch and lost all chance after getting trapped behind horses. Still, he finished a solid fourth, then came back three weeks later and romped in the Derby.

In 2001 John Ward's edge was his unorthodox training of Monarchos. Knowing he would be criticized by the media, he still insisted on giving the son of Maria's Mon several days of inactivity, which consisted of merely walking the shed. He also gave Monarchos his final Derby work nine days before the race. No Derby winner in memory had ever gone into the Run for the Roses with his final work that far out. But Ward realized that Monarchos had turned in such an extraordinary performance in the Florida Derby, the colt was in danger of peaking before the big race. Then the colt was defeated in the Wood Memorial, and Ward was all smiles after the race, knowing he had left something in the tank.

The last thing Monarchos needed during the next three weeks was a hard work. He was sitting on another big effort, and Ward just wanted to keep him where he was. There were several days Ward didn't even show up at the barn, choosing to stay at his farm in Lexington to work with the two-year-olds. The care of the barn and Monarchos' training were left in the hands of his assistant Yvonne Azeff, who had been an assistant to Wayne Lukas, Pat Byrne, and Randy Bradshaw. Azeff had been closely involved with a number of classic and Breeders' Cup winners, and, in a way, she also became Ward's edge. Not many trainers would entrust their assistant with so much responsibility and allow her to make so many important decisions leading up to the Derby.

Two days before the Derby, Ward drove up to Barn 42 at Churchill Downs, played with Monarchos for a few minutes, talking to him as he would a three-year-old child, then hopped back into his van and drove into the infield. He had discovered a great vantage point atop one of the makeshift luxury suites near the three-sixteenths pole. He climbed up the stairs to watch Monarchos school in the gate and have his last serious gallop for the Derby. As he watched Monarchos pulling the arms of exercise rider Bryan

John Ward's unconventional approach paid off with Monarchos.

In Bob Baffert's view, Victory Gallop was the horse to beat in 1998.

Becchia, Ward's confidence grew. He knew he now had a horse who wanted to run; who was champing at the bit. All the days off had put the colt on the muscle at the right time. "Look at him," Ward said. "He really wants to mix it up. That's just what I was looking for."

Two days later Monarchos destroyed his field, running the second-fastest time in Derby history and becoming only the second horse to break two minutes for the mile and a quarter. His time of 1:59 4/5 was two-fifths of a second off Secretariat's track record set twenty-eight years earlier. Ward's edge was his confidence in his horse and his training methods in the face of criticism, and having an assistant trainer who knew the horse even better than he did.

Bob Baffert is one trainer who sizes up his opposition as well as anyone. Very little escapes him. Before the 1998 Derby he stood in the trainer's stand one morning and in the middle of a conversation turned his head toward the track just as Victory Gallop went by. "That horse is looking good," Baffert said. "I think he's the horse to beat." Of course, Baffert's Real Quiet was all out to narrowly hold off Victory Gallop at the finish of the Derby.

But as astute as Baffert is in discussing his opponents' strengths and weaknesses, he never tips his hand about his own horses. His edge is that he knows everything he needs to about the other trainers' horses and they know nothing about his. A perfect example was Silver Charm's habit of bleeding after his works. Word leaked out about it, and when anyone mentioned it to Baffert, he hemmed and hawed and basically said nothing.

After the colt's next work, Baffert concocted a scenario with the veterinarian. As he stated in his autobiography, Baffert told the vet, "Doc, I want you to scope him, but when you take it out, I want you to say, 'It looks good.' And I'll talk to you later about it."

So, the vet announced that Silver Charm scoped clean, then told Baffert in private, "It looked terrible. He bled and he's got mucus." But Baffert knew it was a common occurrence with Silver Charm and assured the vet it was nothing to worry about. He just didn't want others thinking there was a weakness in the steel gray colt's armor.

None of this had anything to do with Silver Charm's winning the Derby, but it is a perfect example of how every little edge is important to some trainers. So keep a close eye on trainers, either firsthand or through daily published reports, and watch for the small details. It shows they're doing everything in their power and using all the resources they've stored up over the years in order to win. And you want to see that competitiveness in a trainer, just as you would a baseball manager or a football or basketball coach who looks for any edge he can. When possible immortality can be measured in inches and feet, it doesn't take much to tilt the scale.

CHAPTER

A Tale of Two Trainers

Neil Drysdale and Shelley Riley had one thing in common and only one thing. They both were making their first start in the Kentucky Derby. Drysdale was a highly respected trainer who had won three Breeders' Cup races — with Princess Rooney, Prized, and Tasso — and saddled other major stakes winners such as Bold 'n Determined and Gorgeous. Riley was an unknown trainer, based at the little county-fair track Pomona in northern California. There are several reasons for telling their story: to show how the Kentucky Derby can make strange bedfellows; to show that even the Derby's strictest rules can be broken on occasion; and to show that anyone's dream can come true on the first Saturday in May...at least almost come true.

Drysdale was a scholarly, proper Englishman who had been training horses for eighteen years and worked as an assistant to legendary trainer Charlie Whittingham. Riley was a "horse crazy" gal from Salinas, California, with degrees in sociology and criminal justice. She had never been around a top-class horse in her life. Drysdale had a reputation for being aloof and sometimes cold toward the media, but he also had an impish sense of humor that many people never saw. Riley, a tall, heavyset woman, had a quick wit and a booming laugh and always had something profound to say.

Drysdale arrived at Churchill Downs in 1992 with his $2.9 million yearling purchase A.P. Indy, while Riley brought her $7,500 auction bargain, Casual Lies. The two colts had met twice, with A.P. Indy winning both times, taking the Hollywood Futurity the year before and more recently the Santa Anita Derby. Casual Lies turned in strong efforts to finish third in both races.

Riley never once called her horse Casual Lies. To her he was Stanley. Drysdale never once called his horse anything other than A.P. Indy. There was nothing to indicate Stanley could beat A.P. Indy, and certainly nothing to indicate Riley could beat Drysdale. But here they were on opposite ends of Barn 41, eyeing each other's horse for the two weeks leading up to the Derby.

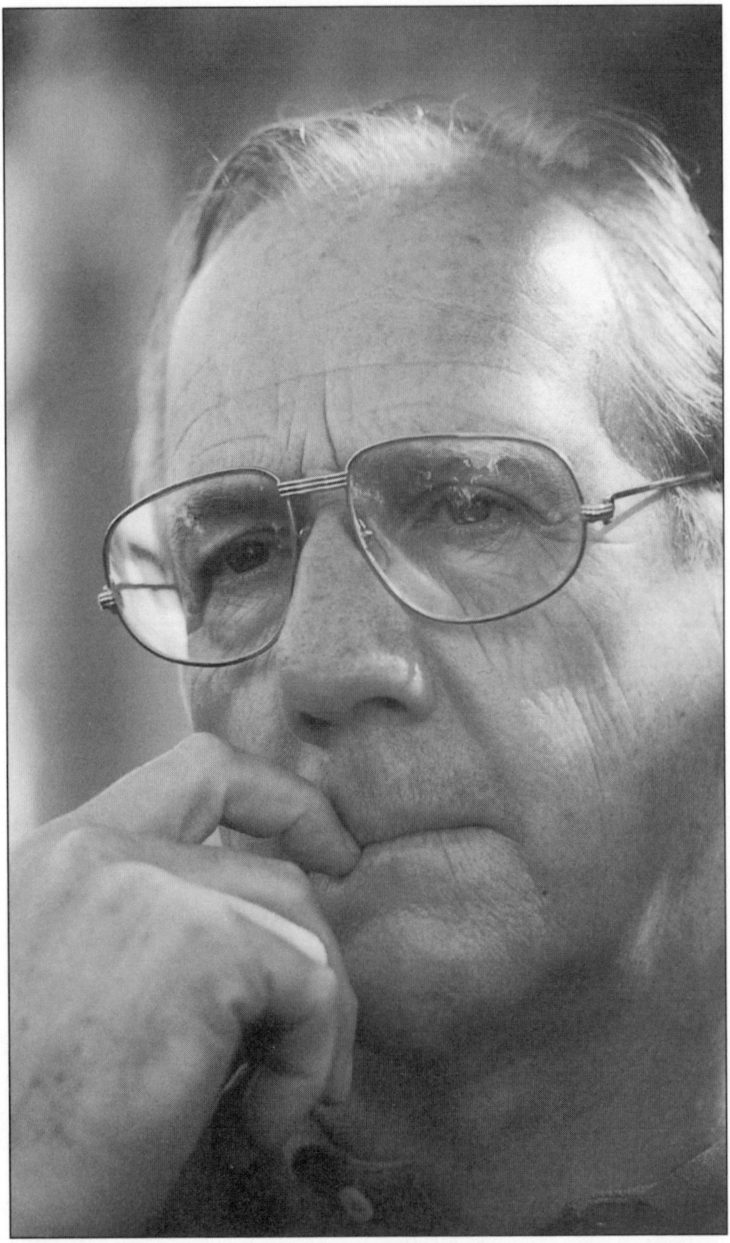

Neil Drysdale had a successful training career well before his first Derby.

The first time they met, Riley was surprised how gracious and personable Drysdale was after hearing all the horror stories portraying him as an "ogre," as Riley put it. Drysdale told Riley he had read that the press found his personality as "cold as a frosty mint julep." But the two bonded as they walked their horses, talked about all kinds of things, and searched the barn looking for stray stones, which for trainers are equivalent to land mines.

Riley described the Derby experience by saying, "If Stanley is the lightning in the bottle, my greatest fear is that if the bottle breaks, the lightning might escape and the chance of a lifetime will pass me by." She knew there was a great deal of cynicism when it came to her and her horse. In her words, the press felt Casual Lies' training and trainer would eventually "catch up to him and the flash in the pan would simmer off into obscurity."

The Derby gremlins didn't waste any time testing the inexperienced Riley. The first week in Kentucky, Casual Lies had an allergic reaction after eating the chemically treated wood shavings in his stall. Riley changed his bedding and treated him for his stomach ailment. Soon, he began to pick up, and his blood count returned to normal. Another day or two of

Shelley Riley and her $7,500 Cinderella horse.

missed training and Riley and Stanley would have been heading back to Pomona.

But he fully recovered and resumed training, breezing a sharp five furlongs in 1:00 flat. Everything was going smoothly for A.P. Indy, who worked to Drysdale's satisfaction. On the Tuesday before the Derby, the French wonder horse Arazi went to the track for the first time. Drysdale paid no attention to the little chestnut with the big entourage, remaining in his office while the colt tested the Churchill strip. When I saw Drysdale later and told him he had missed the big doings, he replied with a straight face, "Oh, I missed it? I was too busy doing the crossword puzzle."

The next day Riley received her first hate letter from someone who was less than pleased that she had taken local rider Alan Patterson off Casual Lies and given the mount to Gary Stevens. The disgruntled fan ended the letter by saying, "We guess the evil dollar came between you and loyalty. It would seem the Cinderella story includes a wicked witch."

Riley had made the switch with a great deal of anguish, especially being close to Patterson and his wife, Nancy. But the Derby is business, not personal. In all, she handled the whole Derby experience like a pro, appearing on countless radio and television shows and becoming a spokesperson for women everywhere. Unlike most inexperienced trainers at the Derby, Riley had her head on straight, and I was amazed at her poise and sense of humor, and how she took everything in stride. She always said the right thing.

I was covering the Derby for the *Daily Racing Form*, and one of my assignments was to do a diary with Riley. This is how she described the scene at the Downs one night when she went back to the barn to "tuck in" Stanley: "The Twin Spires, which are nor-

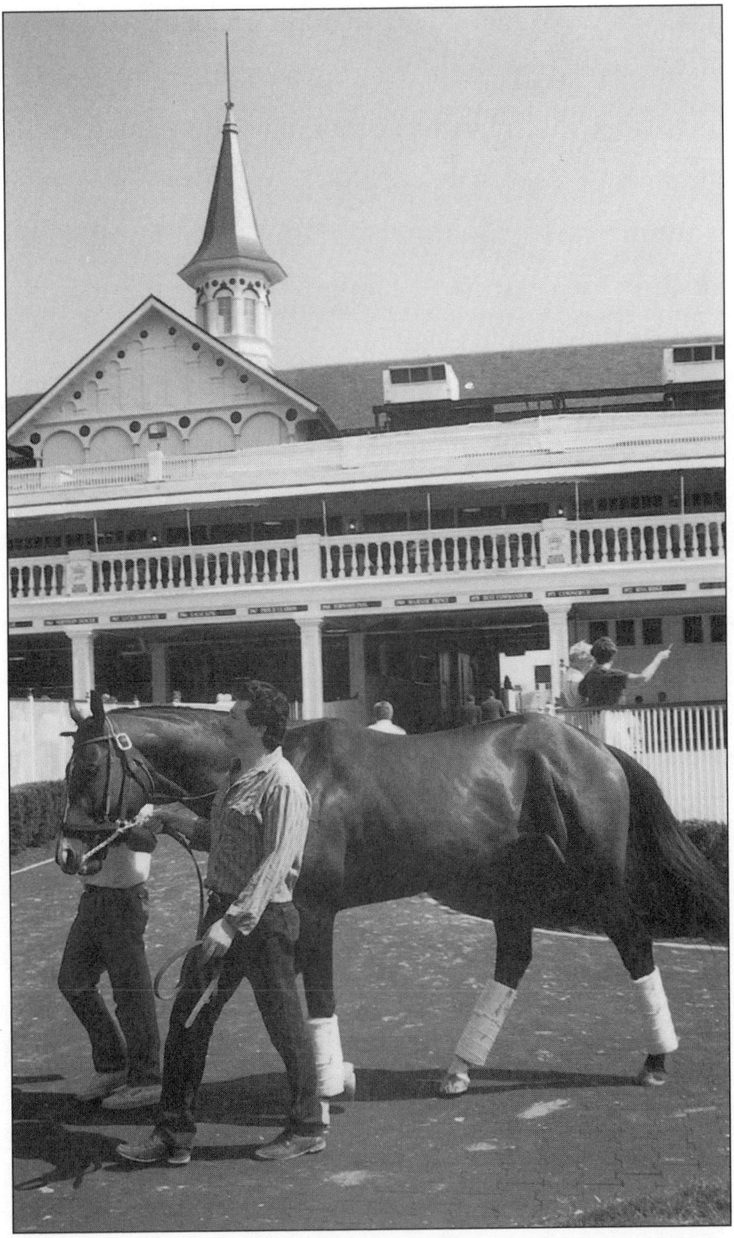

Schooling in the paddock was the closest A.P. Indy got to the Derby.

mally lit every night, had an additional pale blue spotlight trained on each. There was a slight mist in the night air, and it was crispy cold. The mist passing between the spotlights of the Twin Spires made them shimmer ever so slightly, giving them an ethereal quality. I was afraid to blink. I sat there mesmerized in case they would evaporate in the night.

"There is such a feeling of history here. If you listen real close you just might hear the beating hooves, see the steam from the flared nostrils, as one of the greats of the past quickly appears and passes beyond your view. So many this way have passed and so many yet to come. Now it would appear as if history is going to smile on us. Saturday will determine the path our dream will follow — to be fulfilled or dashed. Maybe just being a part of it will be enough. I'll know for sure on Sunday."

At the other end of the barn, however, it was beginning to look as if history was not going to smile down on Drysdale. A.P. Indy had apparently stepped on a stone and bruised his foot. As vets worked feverishly on the colt's foot, no one knew of the injury other than my colleague at the *Racing Form*, Joe Hirsch, who was asked to keep it under wraps until they knew for sure the extent of the bruise and whether it

Casual Lies progressed beautifully at Churchill Downs...

would keep A.P. Indy out of the Derby. It was diagnosed as a blind quarter crack in his left front foot. It wasn't serious, but it needed time to heal with the help of a fiberglass patch.

On the morning of the Derby, with only a smattering of media on the backstretch, Drysdale and A.P. Indy's owner Tomonori Tsurumaki made the official announcement in the recreation room that the colt had been scratched. Both men handled the situation with class and never showed any signs of the disappointment they were keeping bottled up. Drysdale's wife, Inger, was not as strong, as she tried unsuccessfully to hide the tears behind her sunglasses. She removed the glasses and began to weep. Tomonori

...while A.P. Indy's crushed connections scratched their colt on Derby morning.

saw her and went over and embraced her. Inger could do nothing but bury her head in his shoulder. "This business is so cruel," she said, barely able to get out the words. "As blasé as Neil may seem about the whole thing, you know he's not. In all the years he's been training, this is the first time he's come so close. I just wish people had gotten to know him. I guess we'll just pick up and go on."

That afternoon, Casual Lies ran the race of his life to finish second in the Derby. Only Lil E. Tee stood between Riley and her fairy-tale ending. Casual Lies fought back after being passed by the winner, but at the wire, a length separated him and Riley from immortality.

A few hours after the race, torrential rains pounded down on the roofs of the barns, and bolts of lightning illuminated the backstretch. A.P. Indy was oblivious to it all, as he stood by his stall door peering out into the darkness. Outside the stall Drysdale stood alone, with nothing but his thoughts. If there was one thing that Casual Lies' performance proved, it was that A.P. Indy in all likelihood would have won the 118th Kentucky Derby.

At the other end of the barn, a crash of thunder sent Casual Lies charging to the back of his stall. Riley was still over at the Derby Museum's post-race party, and when Drysdale saw her husband, Jim, standing by Casual Lies' stall, he walked over to him.

"Fantastic race," he said with a broad smile, patting Jim on the shoulder. "That was just fabulous. Give Shelley a big hug for me."

Drysdale and Riley had come to Churchill Downs as strangers, from two different worlds, but they left with a common bond. They had shared the gamut of emotions that only the Kentucky Derby can stir. Five weeks later, a patched up A.P. Indy won the Belmont Stakes, while it was Casual Lies who suffered a quarter crack during the running of the race. Shelley Riley's dream had ended. Her beloved Stanley eventually was sold as a stallion to stand in New Zealand, never to be heard from again in this country. Soon after, she divorced Jim and moved to England.

For A.P. Indy and Drysdale, there was more glory to come. A.P Indy won the Breeders' Cup Classic later that year, was voted Horse of the Year, and eventually was inducted into the Hall of Fame. Drysdale and Inger divorced, and in 2000 the trainer was inducted into the Hall of Fame, just months after Fusaichi Pegasus presented him with the blanket of roses most people believed he should have had eight years earlier.

Let this be a lesson to all young, inexperienced trainers who come to Churchill Downs with visions of roses, mint juleps, and immortality dancing in their heads. With few exceptions, you have to work for it and pay your dues. But once in a while the Derby will often let you reach out and caress that elusive moonbeam for a few seconds, only to have it, as Shelley Riley said, evaporate in the night. Sometimes, that has to be enough.

CHAPTER

Riders Up!

It was five days before the 1995 Kentucky Derby and trainer Bruce Jackson was fuming. “We got screwed,” he said disgustedly.

Here is the chain of events that preceded Jackson’s comment. Corey Nakatani is the regular rider of the filly Serena’s Song. Nakatani and his agent, Bob Meldahl, are convinced Wayne Lukas is going to run her in the Kentucky Oaks, the day before the Derby, even though she had trounced the boys in the Jim Beam Stakes at Turfway Park. Meldahl then goes to Jackson looking to ride his colt In Character in the Derby. Jackson, convinced he has a firm commitment, turns down the offers from Craig Perret and Chris McCarron to ride his horse, telling them he’s given the mount to Nakatani.

A week before the Derby, Lukas makes the surprise announcement on ABC that Serena’s Song definitely will run in the Derby. Nakatani and Meldahl are floored. Jackson is shocked. Meldahl calls Jackson the next day and informs him that Nakatani is back on the filly.

"You gotta do what you gotta do," Meldahl tells Jackson. "We feel our commitment is with Serena's Song." Lukas insists he left "a crack open in the door," telling Meldahl he was leaning heavily toward the Oaks, but it "could go either way." Unfortunately for Jackson, both Perret and McCarron have already lined up other mounts for the Derby, and he now has to go searching for a rider after losing out on the two he really wanted. He assigns Chris Antley the mount.

The result of all this chaos and ill feeling: Nakatani finishes sixteenth on Serena's Song; Antley finishes tenth with In Character; McCarron finishes seventh aboard Knockadoon; and Perret finishes fifteenth on Jambalaya Jazz.

Such is Derby life in the world of the jockey and his trusty agent. Let's face it — everyone is trying his best to get every advantage, and the reality is trainers get shafted on occasion by jocks' agents, just as jocks' agents get shafted by trainers. It's business, not personal. Every trainer wants Jerry Bailey or Gary Stevens or McCarron or Pat Day, and all four want to ride the best

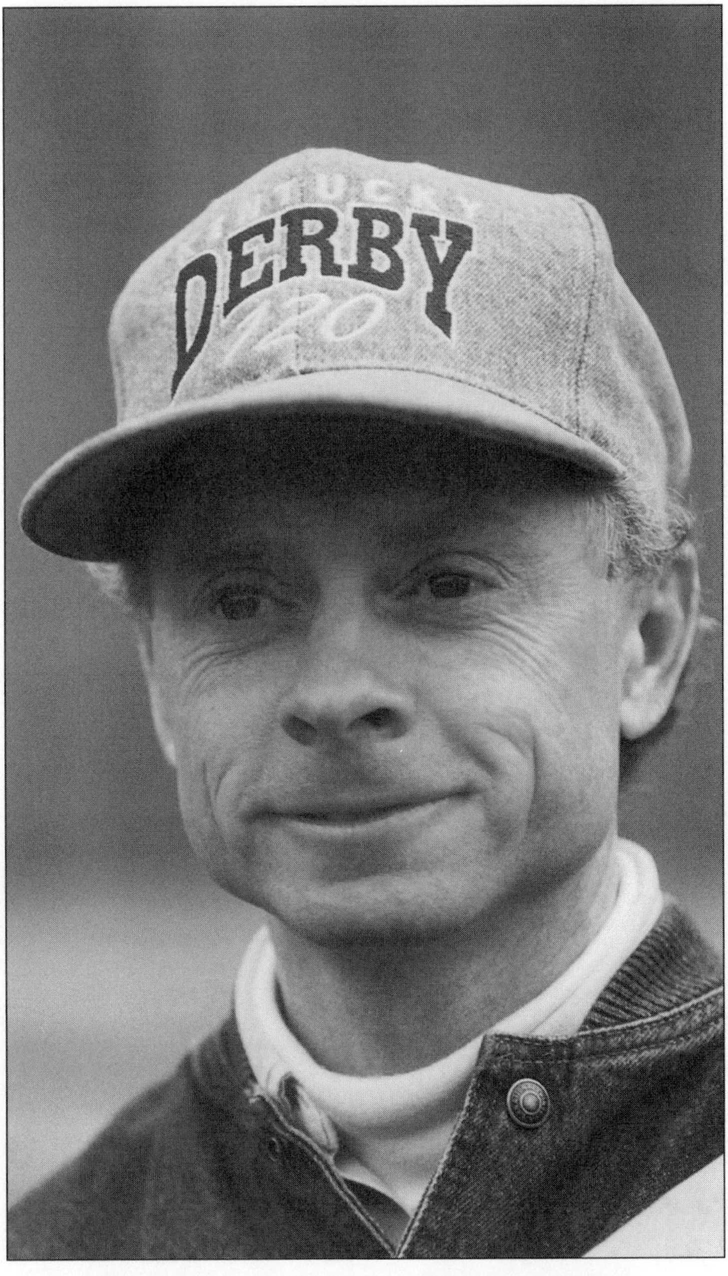

Chris McCarron, as solid a rider as you'll find.

 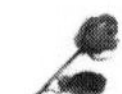

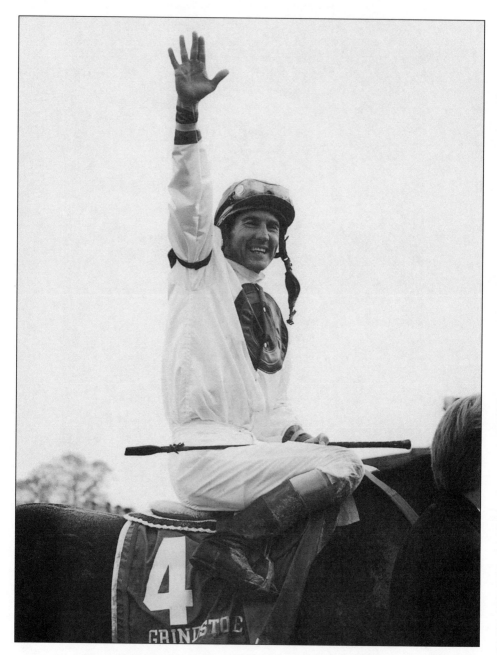

There is no better all-around rider than Jerry Bailey.

horse, so unless firm commitments are involved, something's got to give. And that something can range from begging to bargaining to backstabbing.

Trainers and jockeys are fickle, and no matter how they feel about each other, they cast aside their personal feelings if they have a chance to get the best. In 2001 Bob Baffert said he "begged" Jerry Bailey to ride Congaree in the Wood Memorial and Kentucky Derby, but Bailey and his agent, Ron Anderson, felt Congaree's lack of experience would hurt him in the Derby, so they opted to ride Hero's Tribute in the Blue Grass Stakes, which was the same day as the Wood.

"I was so mad at Bailey and his agent," Baffert said. "After winning the six-million-dollar Dubai World Cup for me (on Captain Steve), you would think I could sway them. It was a stupid decision, and I told them that."

After Congaree won the Wood Memorial and Hero's Tribute finished last in the Blue Grass, a visibly upset Bailey tried to get back on Congaree for the Derby. But Baffert would have nothing to do with him, and stayed with Victor Espinoza. "I told them that bus already left town," Baffert said before the Derby. But when they went to the gate for the Preakness Stakes, guess who was on Congaree? Yep, Jerry Bailey. No

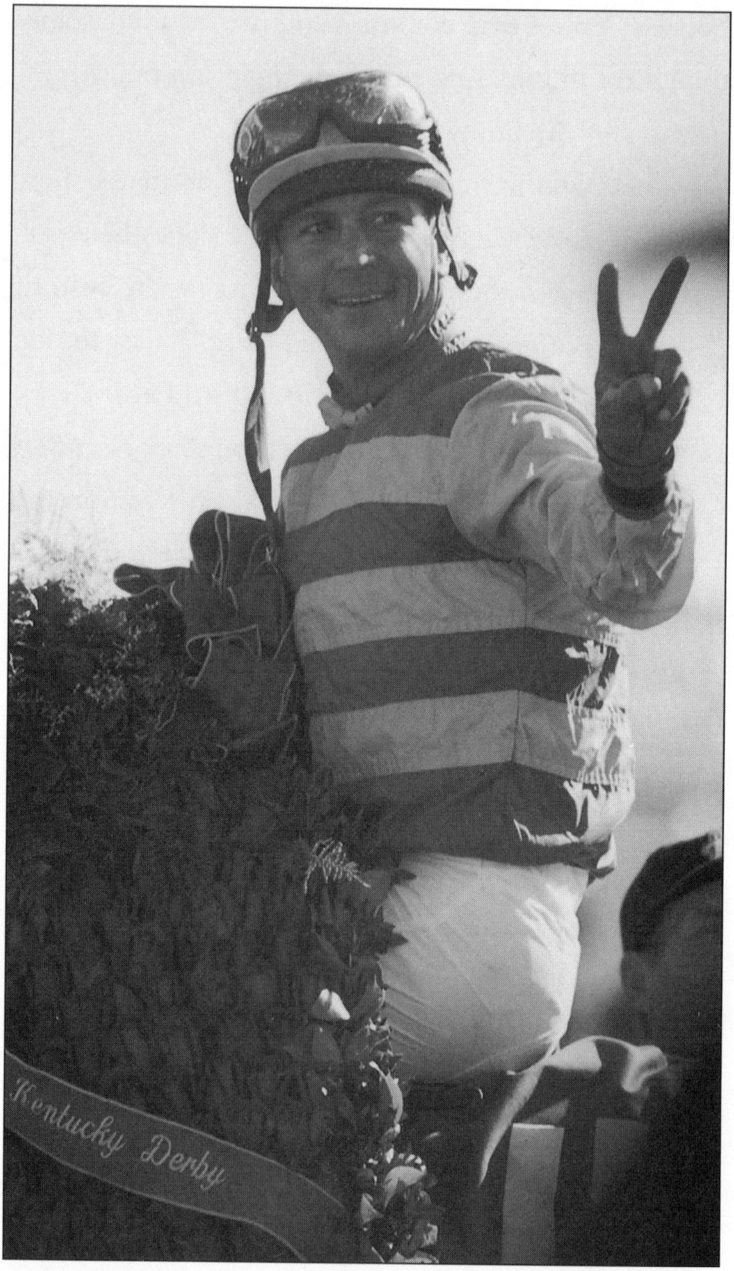

Chris Antley, who possibly saved Charismatic's life.

matter what is said, those buses always wind up coming back.

In 1999 Lukas wanted Laffit Pincay Jr. to ride Charismatic in the Derby. The aging Pincay had not ridden in the Derby in five years and had not come remotely close to winning since his second-place finish aboard Stephan's Odyssey in 1985, one year after he had won it aboard Swale. When Lukas asked Pincay to ride his colt in the Lexington Stakes at Keeneland, Pincay decided he'd rather stay in California to ride several live mounts. No problem, said Lukas. He'd use Pincay in the Derby but Jerry Bailey in the Lexington. Bailey was already committed to ride Godolphin's Worldly Manner in the Derby, so there'd be no conflict.

"The day before the Lexington," Lukas said, "I read in the paper that Pincay had accepted the mount on Event of the Year in the Mervyn LeRoy Handicap at Hollywood Park, the same day as the Derby." So Lukas took a shot with Chris Antley, who was attempting to make a comeback from weight and drug problems. As everyone knows, Charismatic won the Derby and Preakness, and it was Antley who may very well have saved the colt's life after he broke down past the finish line in the Belmont. Antley

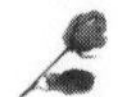

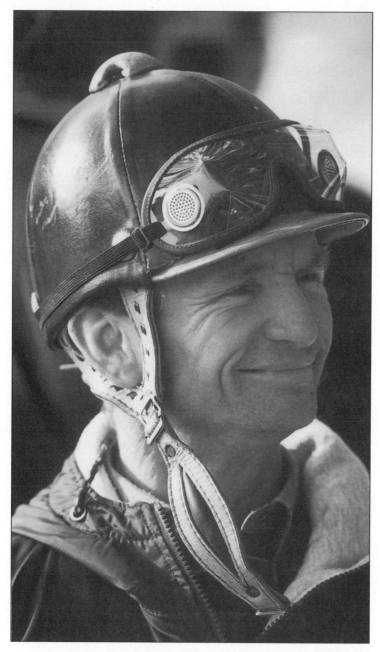

Pat Day's patience often wins races.

pulled Charismatic up quickly, then jumped off and fell over backward. He crawled over to the horse and, sitting on the seat of his pants, lifted the colt's leg off the ground to take any pressure off. So who knows if Charismatic would be alive today if it weren't for Antley's actions and Pincay's taking off the horse.

On rare occasions losing a Derby mount after the Derby can work to the jockey's benefit. Before the 1996 Preakness, Lukas took Pat Day off Prince of Thieves after a third-place finish in the Derby and named Bailey to replace him. Bailey had just won the Derby for Lukas aboard Grindstone, but the colt came out of the race with knee chips and was retired. Nick Zito jumped right in and named Day to ride Louis Quatorze, who had finished sixteenth in the Derby. Day and Louis Quatorze teamed up to win the Preakness, equaling the stakes record.

As I said, trainers want the best and for good reason. Just look at the names of the last twenty Derby-winning jockeys (counting back from 2001) — Jorge Chavez, Kent Desormeaux, Chris Antley, Kent Desormeaux, Gary Stevens, Jerry Bailey, Gary Stevens, Chris McCarron, Jerry Bailey, Pat Day, Chris Antley, Craig Perret, Pat Valenzuela, Gary Stevens, Chris McCarron, Bill Shoemaker, Angel Cordero Jr.,

Corey Nakatani, a strong and daring rider.

Laffit Pincay Jr., Eddie Delahoussaye, and Eddie Delahoussaye. Like trainers, a big-name veteran rider always wins the Derby. You have to go back to Ron Franklin in 1979 to find a young little-known rider winning the Derby, and Franklin happened to be on Spectacular Bid, whom my daughter probably could have ridden to victory.

So always remember to concentrate on the big-name riders for the Derby, and pay close attention to all the melodramas that unfold during the winter and spring, when jockeys are trying to line up their Derby mounts. And as the Derby gets closer, watch for things to get very interesting if one of the upper echelon riders still is without a mount and one of the leading contenders is being ridden by a relatively unknown rider. You can bet the sharks will smell blood and head in for the kill.

However, jocks and agents aren't geniuses. They usually make the right decisions, but not all the time. Don't dismiss a horse simply because a top jockey goes off him to ride someone else, especially if that horse winds up getting another top rider.

The legendary Bill Shoemaker made one major blunder and almost made another. In 1964 Shoemaker took off Northern Dancer after failing to be impressed with the colt's victory in the Florida Derby. He jumped off and onto the big California horse Hill Rise. The rest, as they say, is history, as Northern Dancer, with Bill Hartack up, beat Hill Rise in the Derby and set a new track record. Five years earlier, in 1959, Shoemaker wanted desperately to take off Tomy Lee to ride Sword Dancer, but Tomy Lee's trainer Frank Childs refused to release him from his commitment. At the quarter pole, a tiring Tomy Lee, who was refusing to change leads, came out and bumped Sword Dancer just as the little chestnut colt was about to roar by. Bill Boland, on Sword Dancer, brought his colt back in and returned the favor. But that second bump knocked Tomy Lee onto his right lead and he came on again to nose out Sword Dancer at the wire. So, in this instance, Shoemaker got lucky on two accounts.

Once again we turn to Bailey, who, despite riding Go for Gin to a second-place finish in the 1994 Wood Memorial, decided to jump ship and ride the Wood winner Irgun in the Derby, even though Irgun, like Congaree, had only four career starts. Go for Gin's trainer, Nick Zito, immediately signed up Chris McCarron, who guided the son of Cormorant to a comfortable win, while Irgun had to pull out of the

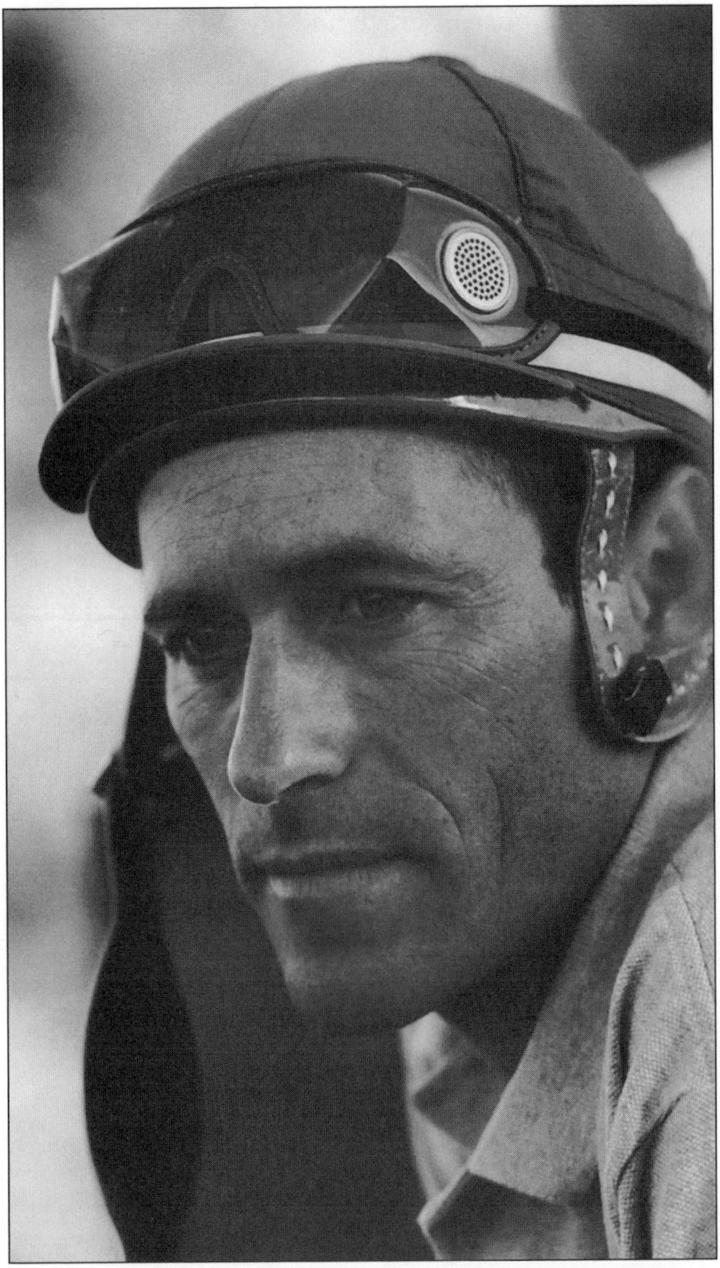

Gary Stevens gets the most out of a horse when it counts.

Derby with a quarter crack and fever. Bailey did land the mount on Blumin Affair, who finished third.

Several years later, McCarron was on the other end, taking off Silver Charm in the Santa Anita Derby in order to ride the Ron McAnally-trained Hello. Gary Stevens got the mount on Silver Charm, then won the Derby a month later and the Preakness two weeks after that. As it turned out, McCarron was injured in a spill and wasn't able to ride in the Derby. He did, however, land the mount on the lightly raced Touch Gold soon after, and wound up stopping Silver Charm's Triple Crown attempt by defeating the big gray in the Belmont Stakes. Oh yes, the rider McCarron replaced on Touch Gold? Gary Stevens. You can't make this stuff up.

While all big-name riders have experience and skill to get the job done, it is also important to remember that certain riders fit certain types of horses. Like buying a suit, trainers should be looking for a perfect fit as much as they should the quality of the material.

There is no better all-around rider than Bailey, and I've yet to find a horse he doesn't fit. Bailey's strength is his uncanny ability to place a horse in the right spot and give him every opportunity to win. If a hole opens, you can be sure Bailey will be there to take advantage of it, as he did aboard Sea Hero and Grindstone. Both rides were things of beauty, especially watching him effortlessly dash through one opening after another on Grindstone. It was as if the race were scripted for him. Many feel Bailey is so successful because he rides the best horses and will do whatever is necessary to land a live mount. Well, regardless of what one may think of Bailey's methods, he's earned the mounts he gets. He rarely makes mistakes, and retaining him to ride a horse is similar to getting Lester Piggott, Europe's king of the turf for so many years. If Bailey's talents are ever compromised, it's aboard classy frontrunners and horses that come from the clouds. There is only so much you can do on those types of horses, and you just have to let them run their race. In short, most good jockeys are going to ride a frontrunner the same way, which takes away some of the advantage Bailey has over the other riders.

If you're looking for an aggressive rider who can wake up the deadest horse, then Gary Stevens is the one you want. Stevens can get more out of a horse in the final eighth than anyone else I've seen since Angel Cordero Jr. He can rate frontrunners and keep closers going for a long while, but his strength is with stalkers. If there's one rider you don't want breathing down your neck, it's Stevens. His rides aboard Silver Charm and Thunder Gulch were vintage Gary Stevens.

Just the opposite of Stevens is Pat Day, whose patience aboard a horse has caused many an anxious moment for bettors and trainers. Day does have a tendency to get a horse in trouble, much like Bill Shoemaker did on occasion, but, like The Shoe, he often uses his patience to win races on horses that would not have won with another rider. Day has soft hands and can communicate with horses. Many times you think he's waited too long, but the next thing you know he's flying down the stretch, getting up in the final yards. The Derby has not been kind to Day. He's won it once with Lil E. Tee, but on four occasions he's finished second — two of them with late runs that came up short. He's also finished third twice aboard closers. In 2001 he had nightmare trips in the Derby and Preakness aboard Dollar Bill. But in the 2000 Belmont Stakes, he gave Commendable a perfect ride, stalking a pedestrian pace, then opening up on the field and pulling off the upset. He's also turned in some super rides in the Preakness, including a brilliant wire-to-wire score on Louis Quatorze. Basically, with Day, you just want to make sure he fits the horse.

The other big-money rider is Chris McCarron, who

Jorge Chavez, who is best on a horse with a sustained run.

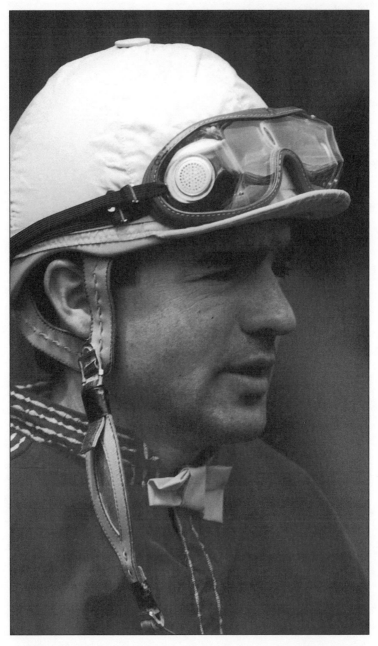

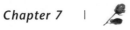

Kent Desormeaux, a young talent with two Derby wins.

has a knack (namely his longtime agent Scotty McLellan) of landing live mounts, and there is no quicker study when it comes to riding a horse for the first time. McCarron is as solid a rider as you'll find, and he's not afraid to take chances. He does like to look behind him a lot and can be punishing with the whip, as can Stevens, but he's a winner. His most notable Derby experience was almost going down aboard Alysheba after the colt clipped Bet Twice's heels shortly after turning for home in the 1987 running. With his quick reflexes and Alysheba's cat-like agility, they managed to recover and go on to victory. McCarron has won a record five Breeders' Cup Classics, all by a half-length or less. Three of them nailed down Horse of the Year honors for his mount. So when the money is on the line, you can't do much better than McCarron.

Let's take a look at a few other big-name riders. Jorge Chavez, winner of the 2001 Derby aboard Monarchos, is short even for a jockey, and he pushes horses a long way out. It's not as easy for him to take a good snug hold of a horse. You definitely prefer him on a horse who can sustain a long run, as opposed to one who likes to be covered up and rated, and then explodes with a quick burst of speed. He's very aggressive, but has learned to relax better with front-runners. Kent Desormeaux and Corey Nakatani can be inconsistent, but they are both very strong and daring riders and will get the most out of a horse. Desormeaux likes to use the reins a good deal, throwing continuous crosses on a horse (crossing the reins to get better balance). He's won two Derbys with horses — Real Quiet and Fusaichi Pegasus — who could turn it on at any point in the race.

This is the top echelon of riders right now, with rising star John Velazquez no doubt sitting on a Derby victory in the near future. If any of these guys approach trainers in March or April wanting to ride their three-year-old, those trainers know they've got a live Derby horse on their hands.

CHAPTER

The Good, the Bad, and the Ugly

In early February of 1941, Ben Jones ran Whirlaway in a six-furlong allowance race at Hialeah, which the colt won by a head in the last jump. Now, there really wasn't anything too unusual about starting the year off running the horse short, other than Whirlaway had run sixteen times as a two-year-old and had progressed to a mile and a sixteenth.

Jones then ran Whirlaway in a seven-furlong allowance race at Hialeah and a six-furlong allowance race at Tropical Park. Whirlaway finished third both times. Upset the colt had failed to sustain his move in each of those races, Jones ran him back six days later in another allowance race, this time dropping him down to five and a half furlongs. When Calumet Farm owner Warren Wright saw Whirlaway's name in the entries again, he questioned such an unorthodox move and confronted his new trainer. Wright felt a five and a half-furlong allowance race at Tropical surely was no spot for a confirmed come-from-behind horse targeted for the Kentucky Derby. Jones stood firm, insisting he knew what he was doing. He was well aware, however, that if this blew up in his face, it could very well cost him his job. Whirlaway wasn't even the favorite in the six-horse field. Still third at the eighth pole, he rallied to get up by a neck, missing the track record by three-fifths of a second.

Wright told Jones after the race there'd be no questioning the trainer's decisions again. And he never did. Whirlaway, of course, went on to sweep the Triple Crown and become one of racing's all-time greats.

Now sixty years later, we have a new breed of owner in the game. Many are businessmen who instead of getting into racing as a sport and a diversion from the corporate world transfer that world to the racetrack. They question trainers and often dictate where a horse will run. Many of them would have canned Ben Jones in a second. It is their money and their investment, and they are intent on calling the shots. There's only one catch with that philosophy — these owners don't win the Kentucky Derby.

Ben Jones did things his way with Whirlaway.

Hiring a veteran, top-name trainer and then overriding his decisions defeats the purpose of getting such a trainer in the first place. Hiring a young, inexperienced "yes" man as trainer is fine for the ego, but that certainly won't win you the Derby either.

It is not merely a coincidence that over the past decade and a half the Kentucky Derby has been won by these owners: John and Debby Oxley, Fusao Sekiguchi, Bob and Beverly Lewis, Mike Pegram, William T. Young, Michael Tabor, William Condren and Joe Cornacchia, Paul Mellon, W. Cal Partee, Frances Genter, Arthur Hancock, Eugene Klein, the Scharbauer family, and Elizabeth Keck. All of them were class owners who had the good sense to hire proven veteran trainers and leave them alone.

Owners today must have it drummed into their heads just how difficult it is to win the Kentucky Derby. Simply investing a lot of money is no guarantee. The Phipps family — the late Mrs. Henry Carnegie Phipps, her son Ogden, and grandson Ogden Mills — is winless in the Derby in eleven attempts. All they have to show for their efforts is a pair of seconds and a third. Cornelius Vanderbilt Whitney inherited one of America's great racing stables yet failed to win the Derby in fifteen attempts, managing only one second and one third.

The list of names goes on and on: Alfred Vanderbilt never won the Derby, nor did Joseph Widener. His son George D. Widener never even ran a horse in the Derby. Max Gluck's Elmendorf Farm was winless in eight attempts, as was Hal Price Headley, one of the great names in Kentucky racing. Raymond Guest never won the Derby. Dixiana Farm never won in nine attempts. Millard Waldheim's Bwamazon Farm never won in five attempts.

John and Debby Oxley let their trainer train — and won.

Those who are privileged to have a Derby horse should remember these names and realize they have a rare opportunity to accomplish something that many of the titans of the Turf and of American society were unable to do.

I've seen decisions on the Derby trail made, not by trainers or even owners, but by racing managers and farm managers. One year the owner's farm manager mapped out an exciting Derby prospect's campaign, with the trainer having little say. And this was one of the most successful trainers in the country. The horse never made it to the Derby.

I have always admired owners who come to Churchill Downs on the first Saturday in May with a Derby horse and are determined to have fun. They know that just getting there is a thrill of a lifetime, so why not enjoy it for all it's worth? Ronnie Lamarque and Louie Roussel of New Orleans came to Kentucky in 1988 with Risen Star, who wound up finishing a fast-closing third. Complete opposites in personality, they complemented each other perfectly. After Risen Star won the Preakness, the brazen, outspoken Lamarque introduced on national TV a song he had written about the horse, to the tune of "New York, New York." Roussel, who also trained the horse, was low keyed and very religious, and was the first one to praise Risen Star for overcoming his lack of training skills. Risen Star went to New York and won the Belmont Stakes by nearly fifteen lengths.

In 1994 the pair returned to Churchill with Kandaly, winner of the Louisiana Derby. Lamarque had written and recorded a song called "Go! Kandaly, Go!" to the tune of Manfred Mann's big hit of the sixties, "Do Wah Diddy Diddy." It was professionally made, with a backup group called Bobby Cure and the Summertime Blues. Each morning Lamarque would invite members of the press to come into his white Lincoln Continental to listen to a tape of the song. The stipulation from Roussel was that for every reporter Lamarque lured in the car, he had to pay Roussel one hundred dollars to be donated to the Little Sisters of the Poor.

One evening during Derby Week, Lamarque and Roussel threw a party on the clubhouse turn, with a large banner reading "Louie and Ronnie's New Orleans Crawfish Bash — Go! Kandaly, Go!" Ronnie was right at home, standing behind a huge vat of crawfish, dishing out the little creatures, and providing instructions on how to eat them.

I had come down with a bad case of pharyngitis

Louie Roussel (right) and Ronnie Lamarque came to Louisville to have fun — and did.

that year and was feeling pretty ill all week. Every morning Louie always had a handful of Luden's cough drops for me. As it turned out, the track came up sloppy on Derby Day and Kandaly was scratched after the fifth race.

Even though Kandaly never even got a chance to run, his name still evokes wonderful memories of that Derby. And all because of two owners who had come to Louisville to have fun and experience the race with the same gusto as feasting upon a plate of jambalaya.

Another owner, Mark Stanley, who had Ecton Park in the 1999 Derby, liked to stand on the track apron. Before a race, he'd just pace back and forth, with a beer in his hand, mingling with the fans. As the horses came charging to the finish line, he'd run alongside them, cheering on his horse. Now that's an owner who enjoys the game. And he was gracious in defeat, which is the sign of a class owner.

You get all types of owners for the Derby, most of them there for the first time. In 1995 Donald Kroeger, who owned Arkansas Derby winner Dazzling Falls, parked his Winnebago on the lawn outside the stable gate and lived there during Derby Week, walking to the track with his wife.

In 2000 Fusaichi Pegasus' owner, Fusao Sekiguchi,

Geisha girls gave the 2000 Derby an exotic touch.

showed up with a bevy of geisha girls in full garb and make-up. Two years before, Madeleine Paulson and Jenny Craig, co-owners of Rock and Roll, brought actor Jack Nicholson as their guest. As Nicholson stood on the track, getting ready for the walk over, he looked as if he had indulged in a few spirits over the course of the afternoon. Being I knew Madeleine pretty well, I attempted to have a conversation/interview with Nicholson, but he could barely get any words to make their way through the frozen grin on his face.

The 1994 Derby was chock full of interesting owners from the entertainment world. There were composer Burt Bacharach with Soul of the Matter, Motown Records founder Berry Gordy with Powis

Castle, and Brocco's owner, Albert Broccoli, producer of the James Bond movies. All of them left their respective empires back home and allowed themselves to be humbled by the Derby's overwhelming presence. Bacharach endeared himself to everyone by saying that winning the Derby would be as much of a thrill as, if not more than, winning an Academy Award.

One word of advice: Owners who come to the Derby with their marketing hat on and start handing out

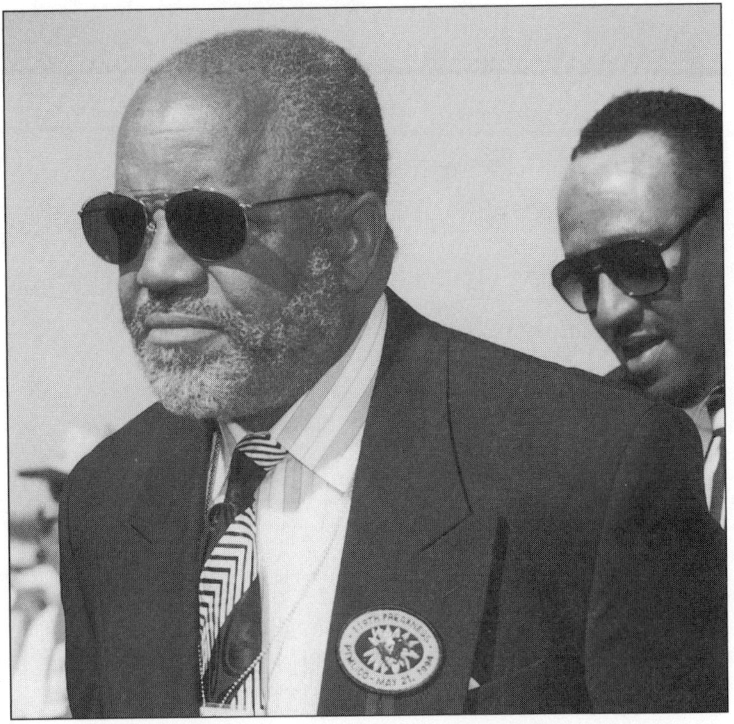

Berry Gordy lent star appeal to the 1994 Derby.

souvenir shirts, pens, notepads, socks, dishes, or anything with their horse's name and picture on it, are in grave danger of offending the Derby gods, who frown upon such commercialistic endeavors.

An owner bringing a horse to the Derby for the first time would be well advised to follow the example of some of the aforementioned. This could very well be the only such experience under the famed Twin Spires, and win or lose, the owner of a Derby horse has an opportunity to leave behind a part of him or herself. What part that might be is for the owner to decide. Or the owner can merely fade into oblivion, leaving not even the slightest trace that he or she was ever there. There is a distinct formula for success that has proven its worth year after year, and following it might give an owner a fighting chance to achieve something that has eluded so many before.

Exposing the Myths

Fact: No two-year-old champion has won the Derby since Spectacular Bid in 1979. Fact: No Breeders' Cup Juvenile winner has ever won the Derby.

Myth or reality? Horses of the past were superior to the horses now. Myth or reality? Winning a final prep for the Derby is the kiss of death. Myth or reality? Wayne Lukas and Bob Baffert, in their quest to make the Derby, are too hard on their horses.

As long as there is a Kentucky Derby, people will take historical trends, their own observations, and their opinions to form personal truisms. But they should know by now that there are no absolutes when it comes to the Derby. Sure, trends can be used in eliminating horses in a handicapping sense, but there usually is a reason behind them. In the past few years, we've seen Fusaichi Pegasus break the trend that favorites do not win the Derby. We've seen Real

Quiet and Charismatic defy the rule that no horse with a dosage index higher than 4.00 can win the Derby. We've seen Fusaichi Pegasus and Charismatic debunk the theory that a defeat is better than a victory in the race before the Derby.

In short, the Derby is a race of mythic proportion, and every concocted rule that pertains to it is mythical.

If you have a two-year-old champion or a Breeders' Cup Juvenile winner, should you keep him as far away from Churchill Downs as you can on the first Saturday in May? There is no doubt that the two titles are correlated, as thirteen of the seventeen Breeders' Cup Juvenile winners (through 2000) went on to be named champion two-year-old. And that is the key to the entire puzzle. It's not that two-year-old champions can't win the Kentucky Derby; it's just that a good number of two-year-old champions should not have been named champions in the first place, and of the deserving champions, many bore no resemblance to a Derby horse.

Just look at all the two-year-olds who were voted champions, based strictly off one race — the Breeders' Cup Juvenile. Did horses like Macho Uno, Anees, Answer Lively, Rhythm, Capote, and Tasso really have true championship campaigns? Did

Juvenile winners with legitimate championship credentials, such as Favorite Trick, Boston Harbor, Gilded Time, and Capote, really look as if they wanted any part of a mile and a quarter?

It's easy to look back to the seventies and see that two-year-old champions Spectacular Bid, Affirmed, Seattle Slew, Foolish Pleasure, Secretariat, and Riva Ridge all went on to win the Derby. But do you know how many two-year-old champions in the sixties won the Derby? None. Do you know how many two-year-old champions in the fifties won the Derby? None. In the forties, during the great Calumet dynasty, there were two. This dearth is not some unexplained phenomenon we're going through. History has shown us it's actually the normal order of things. It is the seventies that is the aberration, partly because so many superstars came along, including three Triple Crown winners and two others who in all likelihood should have won the Triple Crown.

Yes, times have changed from the seventies, and in recent years you're finding more late developers like Monarchos, Fusaichi Pegasus, Charismatic, and Grindstone winning the Derby. Part of the reason is that, unlike past years, we're emphasizing having horses peak in November for the Breeders' Cup. Then we don't give them proper time over the winter to freshen up for a Triple Crown campaign. And, let's face it, whether you realize it or not, it's a lot harder to win the Derby now than it was twenty years ago.

In 2001, for example, of the seventeen starters, thirteen were graded stakes winners, two had won listed stakes, and two had placed in graded stakes. Monarchos, therefore, had to defeat fifteen stakes winners and two stakes-placed horses. Of the nineteen horses entered for the 2000 Derby (there was one scratch), eleven were graded stakes winners, five were listed stakes winners, two had placed in graded stakes, and one had placed in a listed stakes.

It's true that more races are now stakes than in the early seventies, but let's compare Derby fields. From 1969 to 1972, here's a sampling of the horses that competed in the Kentucky Derby: Majestic Needle, winner of one allowance race and a maiden special weight race in twenty-three career starts who was coming off a twenty-six-length drubbing in the Blue Grass Stakes; Royal Leverage, whose only win in ten career starts was for a $10,000 claiming tag; Big Brown Bear, whose only victory in eighteen career starts was in a $15,000 claiming race; Saigon Warrior, whose only victory in seventeen starts was a six-

Spectacular Bid is the last two-year-old champion to win the Derby.

furlong maiden race at Oaklawn Park; Fourulla, a maiden in four career starts; Pacallo, who broke his maiden in a $10,000 claiming race in Puerto Rico, and in his only race in America was beaten eleven lengths in a seven-furlong allowance race; Rae Jet, winner of two of twenty-three starts, who went into the Derby after getting beaten in a $20,000 claiming race at six furlongs and finishing sixteen lengths back in the Derby Trial; and Our Trade Winds, who was beaten seventeen lengths in the Derby Trial, was eased in the Blue Grass, and was beaten eleven lengths in the Arkansas Derby.

I won't even bother detailing some of the other equally inept horses who ran in the Derby during that time. People were outraged when Tincin almost made it to the 2001 Derby. Well, racing fans had to put up with Tincins all the time back then.

Of the fourteen horses Riva Ridge faced in the 1972 Derby, excluding the Puerto Rican horse Pacallo, only five had won stakes. In the Centennial Derby in 1974, only thirteen of the twenty-three starters had won stakes.

Because the depth of competition now makes winning the Derby much more difficult, trainers are afraid to have their horses peak too soon, and they certainly don't want them peaking the race before the Derby. As a result, only three of the past twelve Derby winners won their start prior to the Derby. And those three — Fusaichi Pegasus, Charismatic, and Strike the Gold — all were late developers who had done nothing at two and were just finding themselves that spring. But remember, Charismatic and Fusaichi Pegasus captured two of the last three Derbys. Trends are merely that; they change at any time, so don't eliminate a horse simply because he won his start prior to the Derby.

Fusaichi Pegasus was lightly raced, with only five career starts, while Charismatic raced quite often, having made fourteen starts. In cases such as these, you have to study each horse — how it is progressing and what its needs are. Listen to the trainer (if he is a successful veteran trainer) and try to read between the lines. Is he truly sincere in his positive comments or just spewing out the usual rhetoric? In this case, it was the often-raced horse (Charismatic) who kept improving into the Preakness, while the lightly raced horse (Fusaichi Pegasus) regressed at Pimlico.

Orchestrating an early three-year-old campaign that will get a horse to the Derby in prime form requires skillful horsemanship and expert planning. Over the years trainers have used three traditional routes: Florida, New York, and California, with Keeneland attracting many of the top Florida horses in the spring. Whereas Hialeah and Gulfstream used to offer a wide choice of prep races, the Florida preps now are basically all at Gulfstream, with the Holy Bull, Hutcheson, Fountain of Youth, and Florida Derby. Hialeah, which for years staged the Flamingo, once the premier Florida prep, closed down after the 2001 season. The Tampa Bay Derby provides an outlet for Derby horses who do not want to bang heads with the

Charismatic ran often before winning the 1999 Derby.

big boys. The leading Derby contenders who emerge from Gulfstream often head to Keeneland for their final preps in the Blue Grass or Lexington stakes, with some heading north to New York for the Wood Memorial. The Keeneland races now must compete with the Arkansas Derby. While the Arkansas Derby and Louisiana Derby were virtually meaningless preps twenty-five years ago, they have gained in stature and attract far better horses.

The Southern California preps actually begin with a mile and a sixteenth race, the Santa Catalina, then step back to seven furlongs in the San Vicente, before progressing in distance with the one-mile San Rafael, mile and a sixteenth San Felipe, and mile and an eighth Santa Anita Derby. Horses coming out of the Santa Anita Derby have four weeks until the Run for the Roses, as opposed to three weeks for the Wood Memorial, Blue Grass, and Arkansas Derby.

Regardless of trends, a Derby winner can, and has, come along any of these routes. The killer race in recent years has been the Blue Grass Stakes. Although still considered by many as the most important prep for the Derby, it's become a race you don't want to win, especially in an impressive manner or in a fast time. Seven Blue Grass winners have broken 1:48 for the mile and an eighth, and all seven were beaten in the Derby, although Forward Pass was named the winner in 1968 after a butazolidin positive eventually disqualified Dancer's Image. The other horses who ran faster than 1:48 were Round Table, Arts and Letters, Chief's Crown, Skip Away, Ridan, and Halory Hunter. A star-studded group for sure, but none of them were able to come back and win the Derby. Strike the Gold won the Blue Grass, then the Derby, but his time in the prep race was a less taxing 1:48 2/5. Other Derby winners who successfully used the Blue Grass as a prep include Northern Dancer,

Strike the Gold scored a Blue Grass-Derby double.

who covered the mile and one-eighth in 1:49 4/5, Dust Commander, 1:51 1/5, and Spectacular Bid, 1:50.

One of the reasons not many Blue Grass winners come back and win the Derby is the difference in surfaces between Churchill Downs and Keeneland. Churchill is deeper and more forgiving, while Keeneland, with its coarser sand, can be harder on the feet, especially when it's wet. And nowhere will you find a more speed-biased rail than on certain days at Keeneland. And many of the Blue Grass winners we mentioned earlier who ran fast did indeed win on the front end. It is very unlikely these types of horses will come back in three weeks and win the Derby using those same tactics. Several top-class, wire-to-wire Blue Grass winners of recent years like Millenium Wind, Skip Away, Holy Bull, Chief's Crown, and Proud Appeal never even saw the lead in the Derby.

Churchill may very well be the best-draining track in the country, soaking up water like a sponge, and it is rare that you see the same track on Derby Day that you saw in the weeks preceding the race. One nagging fact that remains in the back of a trainer's mind is that some horses simply do not like Churchill, which is why you see horses such as Louis Quatorze, Skip Away, Point Given, Snow Chief, Hansel, and Tank's Prospect all finish up the track in the Derby, then come back and finish first or second in the Preakness. Whether they all disliked Churchill is open to question, but their dramatic form reversal certainly is not.

The long stretch at Churchill Downs (1,234 feet, six inches) you always hear or read about is overrated. The only horse who really needed the long stretch was Grindstone, who just got up in the final stride to win. It didn't hurt Alysheba, who needed time to recover from his near spill at the three-sixteenths pole. Every other Derby winner since Carry Back in 1961 had the race won by the eighth pole.

And now the myth surrounding winning the race

prior to the Derby. Bob Baffert's two Derby winners, Silver Charm in 1997 and Real Quiet in 1998, both were coming off second-place finishes in the Santa Anita Derby. Monarchos romped in the 2001 Derby after finishing second in the Wood Memorial. Grindstone and Lil E. Tee won the 1996 and 1992 Derby, respectively, after finishing second in the Arkansas Derby. Thunder Gulch captured the 1995 Derby by daylight after finishing a dull fourth in the Blue Grass. Go for Gin was a comfortable winner of the 1994 Derby after finishing second in the Wood Memorial. Sea Hero ran off from his field in the 1993 Derby after a fourth-place finish in the Blue Grass. Unbridled won the 1990 Derby by three and a half widening lengths after finishing third in the Blue Grass. Since 1992 only Wood Memorial winner Fusaichi Pegasus and Lexington winner Charismatic have been able to win the Derby coming off a victory.

So has it now become a no-no to win the race before the Derby? Do trainers actually prefer to have their horses get beat in the prep?

This apparent trend is worth noticing. Maybe trainers are too well aware of the fragility of the modern-day Thoroughbred and are petrified when their horse turns in a career-best effort and monster speed figure in the prep. Charismatic ran in the Santa Anita Derby and Lexington Stakes before winning the Derby and Preakness, all in a six-week period, and was dubbed an iron horse. By today's standards he probably was. Trainers now nurture their horses like delicate flowers to ensure they don't blossom too soon. But before you dismiss any horse coming off a victory, always remember that trends are temporary, and with two of the past three Derby winners having won their start before the Derby, it is possible this trend has ended.

On the human front, is it myth or reality that Wayne Lukas and Bob Baffert are hard on their horses? Lukas, it is said, runs his horses too often and at times where they don't belong. Baffert supposedly works his horses too fast. I'm not going to go anywhere near the question, not having day-to-day access to their barns and training methods. I will say, however, that when any trainer makes a total commitment to excel in the classics, he must do so with the knowledge that more horses than normal are going to fall by the wayside. If Lukas is hard on horses, it's certainly not in the mornings. If he runs his young horses often and above their heads at times, it is because classic trainers have weeded out their stock this way for many years.

Max Hirsch, shown with jockey Eddie Arcaro, was another tough trainer.

There was a time when no one paid any attention to all the Calumet horses Ben Jones *didn't* get to the Derby. How tough were Ben and Jimmy Joneses' horses that did make it to Churchill Downs? They won the Derby with Whirlaway, Citation, Lawrin, Ponder, Hill Gail, and Tim Tam, and finished second with Fabius and third with Faultless. All of them finished first or second in the Derby Trial — run four days before the Derby! Try to imagine Wayne Lukas, or any trainer for that matter, running a horse four days before the Derby. Nowadays most trainers won't even work their horses four days before the Derby.

No one was tougher on his young horses than Max Hirsch. We all know that Hirsch won the Derby with Bold Venture in 1936, Assault in 1946, and Middleground in 1950. But many people who were close to Hirsch say he had to weed out an awful lot of horses to come up with those and other top-class runners. Hirsch worked his youngsters very hard and very fast to see which ones could stand up to it. Those that did became stars. Those that didn't were never heard from again.

That is what happens when you have so many well-bred two-year-olds. You very rarely see a big-name trainer run two-year-olds in claiming races, which means they can run them in only so many races. When you have your sights set on Churchill Downs so early, you've got to find out just what you have. These young runners either can cut the mustard against good horses or they can't. And Lukas, like many of his predecessors, will give them every opportunity to prove they can. No one wants to see horses get hurt, but in racing it's survival of the fittest, and that goes for all levels of competition. Horse lovers and purists try to look away from that aspect of racing, but it's the nature of the game and always has been.

There are occasions when getting a horse to the big race is the only objective. It is like shooting pool and concentrating on just sinking the ball without thinking ahead to the next shot. Case in point: Anyone who was around Grindstone in 1996 knew the colt had bum knees, and it was only a matter of time before they'd give out. Even the colt's groom was overheard the day before the Derby saying, "Knees no good." Do you do what you have to and try to win the Derby at the risk of losing him for the rest of his career, or do you go slowly and try to nurture him and keep him going through his four-year-old campaign? Many owners would take the risk at the chance of winning the Derby and a place in history.

Grindstone, of course, won the Derby and came out of the race with knee chips that ended his career. Most owners would make that trade-off, feeling the rewards far outweighed the price that had to be paid. Whether you agree with it, that's horse racing. Just remember how far the sport has come from the days when big-name owners would have young horses with physical maladies and poor conformation killed rather than invest more money in them.

CHAPTER

Etched in Stone?

As difficult as it is to win the Kentucky Derby from the standpoint of preparation, soundness, and the horse's natural ability, it is even more difficult when you consider the number of historical rules that must not be broken. The equine Ten Commandments of the Derby include the following:

- Thou shalt not run without having started at least once as a two-year-old.
- Thou shalt not have less than five career starts prior to the Derby.
- Thou shalt not have less than three starts as a three-year-old.
- Thou shalt not be cast as the favorite in the eyes of the public.
- Thou shalt not have had thy testicles removed.
- Thou shalt not have a dosage index of over 4.00.

Of course, the occasional sinner who failed to follow

all the commandments still managed to emerge victorious. But these unrepentant runners have been few and far between. The dosage commandment, which we'll get into later, fell hard two years in succession, in 1998 and '99. And in 2000 the commandment regarding favorites also was broken. Others have come close to being broken in recent years, which brings up a good question: should we start thinking of writing a new testament?

The granddaddy rule of them all is having had at least one start as a two-year-old. You have to go all the way back to Apollo in 1882 to find a Derby winner who did not race at two. In the past forty-five years, for example, forty horses have attempted to rewrite the history books. Not only did they all fail, but only three of them managed even to finish in the money. And we're talking about some talented horses, such as Pulpit, Forego, Devil His Due, Big Spruce, Air Forbes Won, Corporate Report, Wavering Monarch, Disposal, and On the Sly.

The reason here is pretty simple. It is asking an awful lot of a young horse to beat the best three-year-olds in the country going a mile and a quarter in May without a foundation. Trainers trying to make the Derby with such inexperienced horses generally rush them to make the race, cramming in too many races in too short a period. The only trainer to have a horse who did not race at two to finish as close as second in the Derby was Charlie Whittingham, who placed in the 1994 Derby with Strodes Creek. So if you think you are on a par with the Bald Eagle, go ahead and give it a try. You'd be wiser to follow Joe Orseno's strategy from 2000, when he passed the Derby with Red Bullet and went on to win the Preakness. Those extra two weeks help a lot more than one might think.

Now we must point out that Fusaichi Pegasus raced only once at two, and that was on December 11. It might not seem like much of a difference, but that one race also gave the colt a fifth career start going

Charlie Whittingham nearly broke a Derby commandment with Strodes Creek.

into the Derby, preventing him from having to break a second rule as well. As it is, he did have to overcome the jinx on the favorite. Also, he was trained masterfully by the veteran Hall of Famer Neil Drysdale, and, take my word for it, very few trainers, if any, would have won the Derby with this colt, despite Fusaichi Pegasus' phenomenal talent.

This same philosophy also applies to the rules about having at least five career starts and three as a three-year-old. It all boils down to foundation, one of the necessary prerequisites for winning the Derby. Sunny's Halo managed to win the 1983 Derby with only two starts at three, but you have to consider that he had had eleven starts at two, including four stakes around two turns, two of which he had won. In addition, the Derby field that year was one of the weaker ones. The big horses to come out of that field — Slew o' Gold and Caveat — were not yet anywhere near their best.

The question is, will any of these rules regarding foundation be broken in the near future? All rules can be broken under the right circumstances. With trainers taking a more conservative approach to the Derby than in past years, you probably will see lightly raced horses like Congaree, Indian Charlie, and Stephen

Got Even eventually break the rule. But until they do, it's wise to be wary of these horses. Even in the best of hands, they still have a lot to overcome.

Now do not confuse having a solid foundation with being overraced.

You can have a Derby starter like Charismatic, with fourteen starts prior to the Derby, or Real Quiet, with twelve starts, and still have a horse that will peak on Derby Day. You just have to know your horse. Charismatic thrived on racing, and, in fact, continued his improvement in the Preakness. However, at the opposite end, it's very difficult to compensate for having too few starts.

And please, do not take quotes from trainers of lightly raced horses seriously. Derby trainers say what they have to — some because they simply want an excuse to get to the Derby, and others because they really do not want to go to the Derby but want to protect the owner who does.

Here are the quotes from a trainer, whom we won't name, regarding running his colt in the Derby with only four career starts and none as a two-year-old. When asked about bucking history, he replied, "It's great. I love it. I know I'll be bringing a fit and ready horse, and that'll be enough for him."

Now, did this trainer really mean what he said or was he saying that for the sake of the owner? Either way, it's simply best not to pay attention to quotes such as this, regardless of who makes them. In fact, it's best not to take too many trainer quotes seriously from February to May. Some guys, like Bill Mott, Frank Brothers, Dick Mandella, and Shug McGaughey, for example, are usually dead-honest and do not look at the Derby through rose-colored glasses. It's also probably why they've never won it and rarely get a horse to the race. But at least they've got their heads on straight and will have a good horse later in the year.

Bob Baffert will be very candid to people he knows personally, but he'll throw the usual standard quotes to the majority of the media. Just listen to the horses he talks up. If he doesn't talk in superlatives about a young three-year-old, chances are you can toss that horse from consideration. Baffert knows who his Derby horses are, regardless of what they accomplished as two-year-olds. Despite their brilliance at two, he never considered Exploit, Forest Camp, and Flame Thrower Derby horses. Baffert uses gut instincts better than any other trainer I've ever seen. Remember, this is a trainer who stopped both his Derby winners after the Belmont and put them away for the year, because he felt that's what was best for them, physically and mentally. Both horses — Silver Charm and Real Quiet — came back and won grade I stakes at four, something that is rare for a Derby winner.

So the bottom line is, when in doubt, go with history. Most trainers only will acknowledge historical trends if they have no bearing on their own horse. Otherwise, they'll give you a million reasons why their horse will be the one to buck the trend. Sure, he's big and strong, has a great mind, and does things like an old pro. I've heard the same words every year.

Clyde Van Dusen is the last gelding to win the Derby — in 1929.

There's nothing wrong with thinking positively, whether it's realistic or not. But that is the trainer's luxury, not the public's.

Now we get to the gelding streak. No gelding has won the Derby since Clyde Van Dusen in 1929. My only advice on this rule is to pay it no attention, especially considering the few geldings that run in the Derby. It wasn't castration that caused Cavonnier to get nosed out right on the wire by Grindstone in 1996, this after being whipped across the face at the quarter pole by the rider of another horse. Being a gelding wasn't the reason Prairie Bayou could only finish a fast-closing second in 1993 after rallying from sixteenth. Nor was it the reason Best Pal was second to Strike the Gold in 1991.

There are different reasons — both physical and mental — why horses are gelded. Some colts may simply be too big and awkward, while others may be too ornery and studdish to keep their mind on being a racehorse. In some cases, being gelded might affect a big, immature type of horse that still hasn't quite put it all together, such as General Challenge or Forego. But basically, the reason why no gelding has won the Derby since 1929 is that there aren't that many of them, and most of them just haven't been that good. That nose by which Cavonnier was beaten was all that separated him from becoming the first gelding to win since 1929 and the first California-bred to win since Decidedly in 1962. When you have a gelding in the Derby, see what he looks like and how he acts. If he's an athletic type of horse with talent and a good mind, just forget he's a gelding.

The most engaging, and humorous, battle between trainers and history is without a doubt dosage. Ah, dosage. Even the mere mention of the word sends a shudder up the spines of trainers with Derby aspirations.

What is dosage you ask? Well, I can attempt to explain the formula on which it is based, but I promise it will sound like some scientist discussing his genetic theories while sitting on a rock in the Galapagos Islands. Briefly, it is based on five categories — Brilliant, Intermediate, Classic, Solid, and Professional, meaning in simplistic terms: sprinter speed, mile to a mile and an eighth speed, excelling at a mile and a quarter, stamina, and more stamina.

The concept of dosage was founded by Colonel J.J. Vuillier, a consultant to world-renowned owner and breeder the Aga Khan, who compiled a list of influential stallions who appeared frequently in the pedigrees of top horses, calling them *chef-de-race* stallions. This concept was expanded upon in the 1950s by Italian pedigree expert Franco Varola, who took notice of the different traits, such as speed and stamina, that these stallions pass on to their offspring. Leon Rasmussen, *Daily Racing Form* "Bloodlines" columnist, brought it to the attention of the American public.

When Rasmussen published a series of columns written by Steven Roman, a petro-chemical engineer and student of Thoroughbred racing and breeding, the dosage theory evolved into a handicapping tool for the Kentucky Derby. Roman had devised a mathematical formula to come up with what he called the dosage index and center of distribution, which he discovered could determine not only whether a horse could get a mile and a quarter, but whether he could do it in May of his three-year-old year.

With the help of breeding expert Abram S. Hewitt, Rasmussen and Roman added American stallions to the list of Europeans awarded *chef-de-race* status. These *chef-de-race* stallions are placed in one or two of the aforementioned categories of a particular horse's pedigree. For example, Mr. Prospector, Seattle Slew, and Northern Dancer are Brilliant-Classic *chef-de-race* stallions, while Buckpasser is just Classic and Round

Table just Solid. This categorizing is based on their influence on speed horses, classic horses, and stayers.

A dosage profile is formed based on the number of *chef-de-race* sires in a horse's first four generations. Points are then assigned to each *chef-de-race* sire, decreasing in number the further back you go in the pedigree. Finally, a formula, derived from those number of points, comes up with a dosage index. If you're totally lost, don't worry about it. Dosage indexes of all the leading three-year-olds are printed up in just about all the major racing publications, including Roman's web site, so let someone else do the dirty work.

It was discovered while computing the dosage indexes of Derby winners going back to 1929, none had a number that exceeded 4.00. Based mainly on the dosage index (DI), Rasmussen picked a number of high-priced Derby winners, exactas, and trifectas in the *Racing Form* in the mid-eighties, and the dosage craze was born.

It drove trainers up the wall. They had no clue what dosage was, nor did they want to know. It was hard enough for them to focus on getting a horse to the Derby. The last thing they wanted to hear was that their horse had no shot because he didn't have the dosage. Trainers who had horses with a DI of over 4.00 dissed the dosage theory as being frivolous and meaningless. But these same trainers changed their tune the following year when they discovered their horse qualified. After breathing a sigh of relief, they proceeded to tell everyone that their horse was bred to run all day, quoting the low dosage numbers. The next year, if their horse didn't qualify, dosage once again was rubbish.

Then Strike the Gold won the Derby in 1991 with a DI of 9.00, and his trainer, Nick Zito, began calling dosage "voodoo." After Strike the Gold finished second in the Florida Derby, the headline of a "Bloodlines" column in the *Racing Form* about Strike the Gold's pedigree read, "No Roses on 'Gold' Horizon." Zito promptly cut out the article and taped it to the wall outside Strike the Gold's stall. That column followed the colt from one track to another, eventually turning yellow and becoming shredded along the edges. It seemed to take on a powerful presence. No one was going to stick pins in any Strike the Gold doll. Of course, when Strike the Gold's sire, Alydar, was subsequently named a classic *chef-de-race* sire it lowered his son's DI below 4.00, thus qualifying him to win the Derby.

The dosage theory rebounded, and for the next six years it held true to form. But in 1998 and '99, Baffert and Wayne Lukas knocked it for a loop, winning with non-qualifiers Real Quiet and Charismatic, respectively. When Baffert came up to the press box following Real Quiet's victory, the very first word out of his mouth was "dosage," as if he had just disproved the theory of relativity. After two consecutive setbacks, dosage was pretty much silenced. Many still use it as a handicapping tool, and rightfully so. It has supposedly worked for sixty-nine of the past seventy-two years, so why totally discount it?

As for Real Quiet and Charismatic, a case can be made for both horses getting a mile and a quarter with no problem. With an influx of young stallions, stamina influences are falling further and further back in a horse's pedigree. More stallions and their sons are now contributing nothing in the way of classic and stamina points, so there is no way to counteract the abundance of Brilliant influences of still-prominent stallions like Raise a Native, Nasrullah, and Bold Ruler.

What all this mumbo jumbo means is that dosage should still be considered a serious handicapping tool when it comes to the Derby. But it is not the sure-fire formula it once was. So, you'll either have to combine your own knowledge of pedigrees or read the so-called experts and judge for yourself whether or not a horse can go a mile and a quarter on the first Saturday in May.

CHAPTER

The Derby Gods

Be forewarned, there will come the year when you do everything right, and it will be for nothing. You can own the best horse, do the best training job possible, or come up with every live angle in your handicapping, and you still will have no shot of winning the Derby.

Those are the years when the Derby gods get involved, and no mere mortal is going to interfere with them when they have their minds set on a winner. Now, no one knows exactly who the Derby gods are or how long they've been in existence, or even what they do to keep busy the rest of the year. To the chosen ones, they are generous in their gifts. To those deemed unworthy in a particular year, they will tease and tantalize, and can be downright cruel at times.

The main recipients of their generosity seem to be the elderly — those veterans of the sport who have persevered for years without being rewarded on the first

Saturday in May. The most obvious case in point is the now-famous 1990 Kentucky Derby. After a decade, people still get goosebumps and become teary-eyed whenever they see a replay of Unbridled's trainer Carl Nafzger "calling" the race for ninety-two-year-old owner Mrs. Frances Genter, who had been in racing for almost half a century, but had never before run a horse in the Derby. It is truly one of the great and touching moments in sports history and will forever be part of Derby lore.

If you were the owner or trainer of the two top contenders Summer Squall and Mister Frisky that year, or even had a big bet on them, you had no shot to win. There was nothing on earth you could have done to defeat Unbridled and Mrs. Genter once the Derby gods had made their pick.

Just like there was nothing you could have done to deny Paul Mellon and Mack Miller in 1993 or William T. Young in 1996 or W. Cal Partee in 1992 or Charlie Whittingham and Bill Shoemaker in 1986. Even to this day, Miller believes divine intervention played a major role in guiding Sea Hero through one hole after another and on to victory. You can only hope that whenever it's your turn to have a strong Derby contender, it's a year when the Derby gods have no rooting interest and let the cards fall where they may.

Frances Genter and Unbridled — one of racing's most touching stories.

To relive that memorable scene in 1990, we go back to Churchill Downs and thank the stars, or should we thank the Derby gods, that ABC decided to put a camera on Nafzger and Mrs. Genter. This is what the world saw and heard, as Nafzger, watching through binoculars, provided a play-by-play description of the race to the petite Mrs. Genter:

"He's up to third."

"He's taken the lead," his voice rising to a furious crescendo. Mrs. Genter utters an emotional "Oh," as she brings her tightly squeezed hand up to her mouth in joy and disbelief.

"Come on, Unbridled. He's taken the lead. He's taken the lead." Mrs. Genter's fist is still clenched, pushing against the corner of her mouth, as she tries in vain to see what's happening on the track.

"He's on the lead, Mrs. Genter; he's on the lead." Mrs. Genter's fist opens, and she covers her entire mouth with her hand.

"He's gonna win. He's gonna win. He's gonna win. He's gonna win. He's a winner. He's a winner, Mrs. Genter! There he goes, right there. He's a winner, Mrs. Genter."

Nafzger gives her a kiss. "We won it! We won it! You won the Kentucky Derby! Oh, Mrs. Genter, I love you." He kisses her again.

Now, how in the world were you going to beat Unbridled that day? After seeing this scene, it would have been blasphemous to utter words of displeasure about losing. The Derby gods remember.

Bob Baffert took his heartbreaking nose defeat with Cavonnier in 1996 with dignity and good humor, despite being duped into believing for a brief moment that he had won. Although he was devastated, he never felt sorry for himself and continued through the Triple Crown with Cavonnier, who wound up suffering a bowed tendon in the Belmont Stakes.

Even Baffert couldn't help but feel good for William T. Young, who beat him out in the Derby with Grindstone. He realized Young had paid his dues, and this was his year. Baffert handled everything in an uplifting manner, and it didn't go unnoticed by the Derby gods. The following year, although they made him sweat for it, they rewarded him and the gracious owners of Silver Charm, Bob and Beverly Lewis. They even let him win it again the year after for Mike Pegram, his close friend who had gotten him started in Thoroughbred racing.

Bob Baffert had a feeling Real Quiet would win the Derby for Mike Pegram.

As early as January of Real Quiet's three-year-old season, Baffert was convinced he was going to win the Derby for Pegram. Just get a load of this script that the Derby gods concocted. While on the winner's podium, accepting the trophy for Silver Charm's victory, Baffert proclaimed on national TV: "I want to thank Mike Pegram. Without him I would have never been here." He then turned to Pegram and said, "You got me from the Quarter Horses and told me to come try Thoroughbreds. So, Mike, this is for you, my man."

The next morning Pegram went to the airport to catch a morning flight and was arrested for attempting to carry a weapon aboard the plane. A female friend had given him a wrapped gift the night before and told him to open it before he left. But Pegram forgot about it and just threw it in his case. It turned out to be a gun. When Baffert was informed of Pegram's predicament, he turned to Julian "Buck" Wheat, Churchill's director of horseman's relations. Wheat contacted a friend of his, Captain Steve Thompson of the Louisville Police Department. Thompson went down to the airport and got Pegram released. The two hit it off, and the last thing Thompson said to him was, "The next time I see you will be in the winner's circle after you win the Derby."

Also at that time, Baffert was asked by *The Blood-Horse* magazine to choose a young horse to showcase for a video on conformation. Baffert chose an unraced two-year-old named Real Quiet, whom he had bought as a yearling for only $17,000. Baffert brought the horse out and went over his conformation, discussing all the pluses and minuses and why he and the McKathan brothers were able to see past the colt's crooked legs and narrow frame.

In early January of the following year when Baffert won a small stakes race at Santa Anita called the Run for the Roses with a Mike Pegram-owned horse, that was the icing on the cake. Between his tribute to Pegram, the Captain Thompson episode, the video, and this latest victory, there was no way all this was simply coincidence. "The Derby gods are telling me I'm going to win the Derby for Mike," Baffert said the day after the Run for the Roses. "I really feel it in my gut."

So, did the Derby gods, in a rare act of generosity, reveal their intentions so far in advance? Or were they just putting one over on Baffert to keep him humble? The 1998 Derby did indeed have Real Quiet's name on it. But after two straight wins, Baffert began to get a little too sure of himself, which didn't sit too well with the head honchos upstairs. Never, ever believe the Derby is yours simply because you have the best horse. Over the next three years, they dusted General Challenge, Point Given, Congaree, Prime Timber, Captain Steve, and Excellent Meeting. Only time will tell how long Baffert will have to wait to convince the gods he will never again take the Derby for granted.

In 1999 the Derby gods came out of winter hibernation looking for a worthy winner of the 125th Run for the Roses. When nothing struck their fancy, they decided to make it a reunion of past Derby winners. Chris Antley, who had won aboard Strike the Gold in 1991, had gone through several years of hell, battling drug and weight problems. Despite ballooning right off the jockey weight charts, he was determined to make it back, undergoing a strenuous exercise and dieting campaign. The Derby gods, recognizing this dedication, did some juggling and somehow got Antley up on the back of Charismatic for the Derby.

Charismatic's owners, Bob and Beverly Lewis, had won with Silver Charm only two years earlier, but Bob Lewis had emerged as one of racing's biggest boosters, continually praising the sport in a sincere and articulate manner. When he lost his big three-year-old, Exploit, early in 1999, he took it with a smile. The only reason the Lewises still owned Charismatic that spring was because of free tickets Bob Lewis had given trainer Mike Mitchell for a National Hot Rod Association drag race. When Lukas dropped Charismatic into a $62,500 claiming race in early 1999, Mitchell was all set to claim the son of Summer Squall. But because of the free tickets Lewis had given him he couldn't go through with it.

Three days before the Derby, Wayne Lukas was visited by twelve-year-old Libby Oliver, the daughter of Louisville veterinarian Kurt Oliver. Libby idolized Lukas and was determined to use her uncanny ability to find four-leaf clovers to help out her hero. She walked onto the grassy area along Longfield Avenue and a few seconds later had her good-luck charm. She hurried back to the barn and handed it to Lukas, who tucked it away in his wallet.

On Derby morning Overbrook Farm's yearling manager, Bruce Jensen, paid Lukas a visit, along with his wife and their nine-year-old daughter Kenzie, who was recovering from leukemia following a successful bone marrow transplant. When Kenzie asked Lukas if there was anything she could take to the track and hold for good luck, the hardened veteran trainer couldn't believe the coincidence. He wrapped the

W. Cal Partee had a Derby with his name written on it.

four-leaf clover in paper and stapled the ends, then gave it to Kenzie, who kept it clutched in her hand as Charismatic stormed to victory.

Now, come on, how in the world was Charismatic going to lose that Derby? When the Derby gods work that hard you know their efforts are not going to be in vain.

In 1992 it was eighty-two-year-old W. Cal Partee, a longtime supporter of racing, who was rewarded, along with born-again Christian Pat Day, who had turned to higher authorities after conquering drugs. By bringing home Lil E. Tee, the Derby gods even went against their practice of throwing out horses with bad Derby names.

There are other stories, like Gary Stevens' victory in 1995 aboard Thunder Gulch. Watch the replay of this race and notice how one horse after another seems to disappear in a puff of smoke as Stevens makes his way from the sixteen post all the way across the track, settling comfortably in the two-path going into the first turn. Three days before the Derby, Stevens' close friend and supporter for many years, publicist Mark Kaufman, died suddenly of a heart attack at age

Kent Desormeaux's victory aboard Fusaichi Pegasus was preordained.

forty-seven after attending the annual owner and trainer's dinner in Louisville. On the eve of the big race, Stevens told Kaufman's widow, Molly, that he was going to have "a special passenger with me tomorrow." Whoever or whatever cleared the paths for Thunder Gulch that day, Stevens said after the race, "I felt like I had an angel on my back today."

In early 2000 Kent Desormeaux and his wife, Sonia, were told that their youngest son, Jacob, barely a year old, was deaf. With a heavy heart, Desormeaux went out and won the Kentucky Derby with Fusaichi Pegasus. As he returned to the cheers of the crowd, he couldn't help but think that this was something his son might never hear in his life. Today, Jacob no longer is deaf.

The point of all this, and you can take it anyway you like, is that sometimes things happen in the Derby that are difficult to explain and go beyond handicapping and workouts and other earthly matters. Now, I'm not trying to convert anyone into some bizarre religious belief that there are powers of the spirit that on occasion rule over the Kentucky Derby. But as a writer, or even just a fan, isn't it more fun to believe that there are?

CHAPTER

What They Say, What They Mean

From January until Derby Day you will be overwhelmed by a morass of trainer quotes — in your local paper, trade journals, and on various web sites. Now, you have to remember that trainers, for the most part, speak their own language. It is basically a cliché-laden series of phrases that are used mainly to ward off Turf writers who are nosing around, inquiring about the well-being of the trainers' Derby horses. The belief is that Turf writers, happy to obtain the trainer's latest words of wisdom, will go away satisfied and convinced they have achieved their objective.

Sometimes trainers will even change the phrases around, just so no one will think they're being repetitious. For example, one day a horse returning from a workout or a race "wouldn't blow out a match." The next time, it "wouldn't blow out a candle." Just for the record, there is no difference between the two. This is one of many optimistic terms used by trainers. But these terms have little meaning if universally used. If you could hear a trainer say once in a while his horse returned from a workout so tired it was gasping for air, then the antithesis of that comment might be more meaningful.

What I'm going to do now is provide a glossary of trainers' terms to give you a basic idea of what they say and what they *really* are saying. This possibly will help you in determining just how a particular Derby horse actually is doing. It might even help trainers evaluate their horse realistically if they really thought about what they're saying. But in the trainers' defense, they normally are not free to spout out the truth about a horse whose owner is determined to keep it on the Derby trail. That owner doesn't want to hear bad or even slightly discouraging news, so you can be sure you won't be hearing it either.

He's the best horse I've ever been around: That bold comment usually is made, not by a Lukas, a Drysdale, or a Mott, but by a trainer whose biggest victory came in the Bucharest Stakes at Sam Houston Race Park. The only way to answer that statement is, "So what?" Don't get too carried away when you hear a trainer say that, unless he's a top-name horseman who normally refrains from making those types of comments.

I wouldn't trade places with anyone: This comment is ingrained in the brain of every trainer. Trainers say it so often and with such conviction, you actually find yourself believing them for an instant. Now if you firmly believe they'd rather have their horse than the 2-5 undefeated favorite, then feel free to take them seriously. If you firmly believe they'd rather have their son of Phone Trick or Gilded Time in the Kentucky Derby than the son of A.P. Indy or Seattle Slew, then feel free to take them seriously. Trust me, most trainers who don't have the favorite or second choice would, if given the chance to trade places with "anyone," jump at it in a heartbeat. Now there are some trainers who truly love their horses and wouldn't trade places. If Neil Drysdale says it, believe him. If Bob Baffert says it, believe him. But, you know what? I have never heard either of those guys ever say it. Those are the ones I'd believe if they ever do.

He came off the track bucking and squealing: The truth of that statement is that the horse probably was feeling good to some degree coming off the track. However, the chances that he really was bucking and squealing are pretty remote. Actually, I'm still waiting to witness that rare combination of video and audio from a horse as he comes off the track.

The farther he goes the better he'll get: Many trainers think that if a horse is closing at six furlongs, he'll like seven furlongs even more. If he's closing at a mile and an eighth, he'll love a mile and a quarter. It just doesn't work that way. Most trainers simply are lousy handicappers. The other variation of that comment is, ***"He acts like he'll run all day."*** Okay, so forget that he's by a sprinter out of a mare by a sprinter. He somehow acts like a distance horse — however it is a distance horse acts — and he was closing at six furlongs. Comments like this are not made to deceive in any way. Hopes and dreams have a way of making people believe the unbelievable. All you have to do is look at a horse's pedigree and physique, put two and two together, and you'll have an idea whether or not he wants to run all day. Just remember the words of "Sunny" Jim Fitzsimmons, who when asked before the Jockey Club Gold Cup if his horse could go two miles, answered, "Sure he can go two miles. I just don't know how long it's going to take him."

I didn't want him to go that fast, but he did it easily: What that often means is, "I didn't want him to go that fast, but the exercise rider said he did it easily so I wouldn't hang his hide on the hay rack for screwing up the work." Fast is fast, and a good trainer will know when a track is playing very fast in the morning. It's rare when a top-class trainer is surprised by a workout. By February and March they should know their horse and how it likes to work. And yes, there are some horses who work fast and do it easily, but they are pretty special. The main thing to learn from this comment is that a trainer is allowed so many "I didn't wants" during a Derby campaign. If it becomes too common, there's something amiss, and you might be wise to start looking elsewhere for your Derby horse.

He's matured physically and mentally from two to three: That's good, except horses, like all creatures, are supposed to mature mentally and physically. In cases like this, look for extremes and for true enthusiasm in such comments. For example, if a successful, level-headed trainer enthusiastically says something like, "I can't believe how much more professional he is and how much he's developed physically," you can make something out of it. Otherwise, it's only important if a horse *doesn't* mature from two to three, and it's very rare a trainer will tell you that. Some, like

Mott and Frank Brothers oftentimes will, so know your trainer.

It was a blessing in disguise (at times preceded by the word *maybe*): This comment usually refers to an injury or an illness early in the year, and is the only comment trainers can make to prevent themselves from standing on the roof of their barn and unleashing a barrage of four-letter words. There are blessings in disguise, but you usually aren't aware of them until at least six months later. A *perfect* road to the Derby does not exist. Getting to the Derby does not come without obstacles of some sort. When one of these obstacles does block your way, it is never a blessing (in or out of disguise), at least in relationship to the Derby.

I have to discuss it with the owner: In many cases, again depending on the trainer, that usually means, "I have to ask the owner what he wants to do, because I have no say in the matter." When top veteran trainers say discuss, they mean discuss. When young, inexperienced trainers say it, it could very well mean they're just following instructions. This is the time you want to do a check on the owner to find out the *modus operandi*. Keep away from horses whose owner calls the shots.

He didn't like the track: What that really means is, "I hope he didn't like the track."

Some trainers consistently have classic lines, but Nick Zito stands alone in that department. Zito has an outlook on the Derby all his own, and his comments and analogies fall somewhere between Will Rogers and Yogi Berra. He once said of Suave Prospect, "He doesn't look like he's supposed to make it, but neither did Abraham Lincoln." On another occasion he said of the same horse, "We're on the right side of town. He could be like Steve Young, who waited on the sidelines until it was his turn." Of outsider Crary: "Either the Derby is on the agenda or it's not." On Louis Quatorze's fourth-place finish in the Florida Derby: "I'm done with spring training; now it's personal." On Go for Gin after getting Jerry Bailey to ride him in the Wood Memorial: "I got blue skies and am cruising at 37,000 feet." On Diligence after arriving at Keeneland: "Just the other day, Diligence actually spoke to me. He said, 'Nick, I really like it here at Keeneland; please don't send me anywhere.' That's the first time a horse ever spoke to me."

Then, of course, there is always that one dream quote that makes you sit up in your chair and wonder if you just heard what you thought you did. What a wonderful world it would be if all quotes were as honest as the one I got one year from Tony Reinstedler, who said after his colt War Deputy finished sixth in the 1994 Risen Star Stakes: "We stunk it up pretty bad."

CHAPTER

Dawn at the Downs

The ringing of the phone reverberates against the walls of Room 213 at the Executive Inn Hotel — yes, I stay in the same room every year. I reach over with a rubbery arm, pick up the receiver, and slam it down. Seconds later, a cacophony of garbled music explodes from the alarm clock. The same arm stretches again and turns it off. On most mornings, both of those tools in the waking process are moot because I somehow always seem to wake up minutes before my morning serenades.

It's 4:30 a.m., pitch black out and quiet at that hour. Thoughts begin running through my head: Who is working today? Whose barn should I make sure I visit today? Is it raining? Where am I having dinner tonight and with whom? Should I have grits in the track kitchen or back at the hotel?

I have no recollection of finishing my transcribing

from the night before, so I look at the open page on my legal pad. It reads: "I love the way he galloped out, and the way he came bouncing opf tje twicl..." Darn, I fell asleep again in the middle of transcribing from my tape recorder, which likely is buried somewhere in my bedspread, along with my earphones and pen. No wonder the lights are on and basketball players are running across my TV screen. Is there an hour of the day that ESPN's "Sportscenter" is not on?

The important thing is that it is a new day, with new discoveries, new horses to observe, and new quotes from trainers, exercise riders, and grooms. Heck, even when it's just the same old horses and people, it's still morning at Churchill Downs, and you can never get too many good quotes or soak up too much atmosphere.

I arrive in Louisville two weeks before the Derby, and I basically follow the same routine every day. The first week is relatively peaceful, meeting the trainers — old and new — and seeing many of the Derby horses for the first time working, galloping, and grazing. It's the time when you're really close to the participants. The seeds are planted. Everything is new, except the pizza I order from room service almost every night. It's amazing how I feel as if I were just

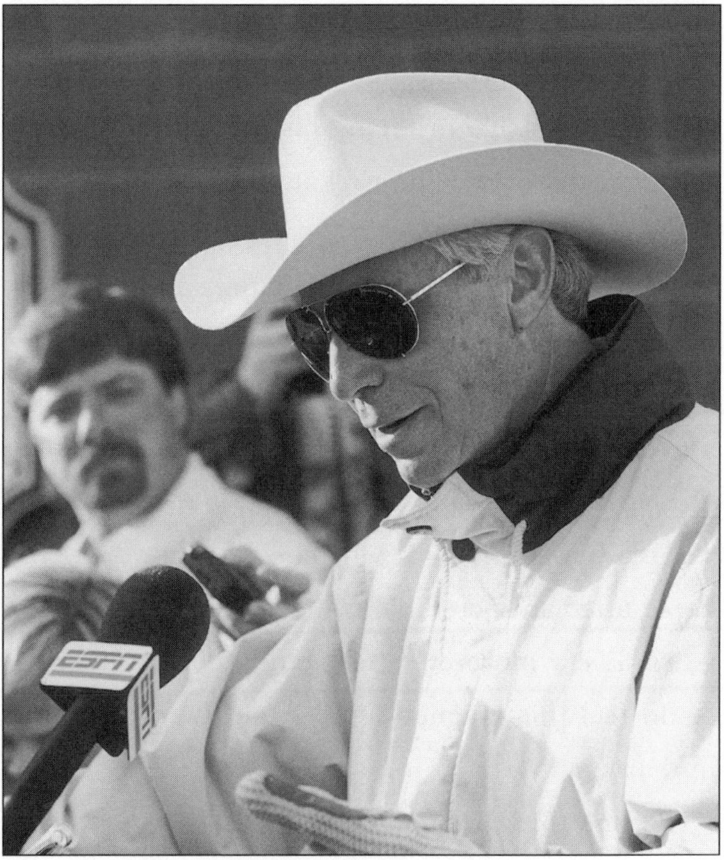

The author usually visits Wayne Lukas first.

here. As I stroll by the Derby barns, a look into each stall can't help but jog my memory banks of Derbys past. Everything at first is slightly out of whack. Hey, what's Thunder Blitz doing in The Deputy's stall? I see Millennium Wind in his stall, but Fusaichi Pegasus is supposed to be in there. Neil Drysdale should be coming out of that office, not David Hofmans. Okay, the initial shock has worn off. The old faces are fading. Time to dive into another Kentucky Derby. In two weeks a new page in racing history will be written. Which of these heads peering out their stall will occupy that page?

My first stop usually is at Wayne Lukas' barn, because Wayne is usually the only trainer there at 5:45. By 6:30 his Derby horse (or horses) is finished for the morning. Plus, Wayne always has something interesting to say and is accessible between sets. It was really weird in 2001 when he didn't have a Derby horse after an incredible run of twenty consecutive years. Every morning, after getting out of my car, I could feel this magnetic pull from the direction of his barn.

The one thing I love about Lukas is that he's the only trainer who will cast aside his fancy clothes and fancy furnishings and fancy belt buckles and get down and dirty with the commoners. If you disagree with Wayne's assessment of any of his Derby horses, he takes it right into the street and dares you to put your money where your mouth is. And he makes the bet so outlandish, it's hard to say no. In 2001, well before the Derby, he offered to bet me any one of his Derby hopefuls horse for horse against any ten three-year-olds of my choice from the Derby list I compile every week. Now, I know it was like taking candy from a baby, but the five hundred bucks he proposed was out of my league, so I crawled away in defeat. Besides, others have fallen prey to Lukas' bets in the past.

Five hundred bucks wasn't out of the league of then *New York Daily News* reporter Bill Finley, who was foolish enough to tell Lukas he liked Jumron in the 1995 Kentucky Derby. Lukas had the favorite, Timber Country, who looked to be a weak favorite after plodding along in his races at Santa Anita, coming away with nothing more than a second, a third, and a fourth. Lukas offered Finley a wager (perhaps dared is a better word): Jumron vs. Timber Country, horse against horse.

"How about fifty dollars?" Finley asked.

"That's not good enough," Lukas said. "It won't make you bleed. Let's make it five hundred."

Finley took the bet, and Lukas wound up winning the Derby with Thunder Gulch, while Timber Country came from far back to nail Jumron by three-quarters of a length for third. The next day, Finley showed up at Lukas' barn with an envelope containing twenty-five twenty-dollar bills.

"I have to say, Wayne never rubbed my nose in it or made me feel bad," Finley said. "I really feel the guy is some mystical spirit who can control these kinds of things. I have no power to combat something like that."

In 1999 Lukas had two Derby horses, the highly regarded Cat Thief and the late-blooming former claimer Charismatic. Ronnie Ebanks, the agent for jockey Shane Sellers, knew he could goad Lukas into making a stupid bet by knocking Charismatic, whom Lukas had been touting big-time. He knew Lukas well enough to realize a betting proposition would be forthcoming. Sure enough, Lukas offered to bet Ebanks two thousand dollars, horse against horse, Charismatic, one of the longest prices in the field, vs. Sellers' mount, Vicar, winner of the grade I Florida Derby and Fountain of Youth Stakes, and one of the leading contenders.

The always happy-go-lucky Ebanks accepted the bet, then burst out in laughter, having led Lukas into a major sucker bet. The following morning, Ebanks returned, still grinning like the Cheshire cat. "I'm sure you came to your senses this morning and realize you're in a financially bad situation," Ebanks told Lukas.

"No, no," Lukas replied. "I don't catch a soft touch like you every day."

Ebanks had Lukas right where he wanted him and kept jabbing in the needle. "I led you right into my trap," he said. "I got you fired up, and I know if you get fired up, that's the best time to get you in a bad bet. So, let's get this straight, we've got a two-thousand-dollar bet, horse for horse, whoever finishes in front of the other, Vicar against...how do you say your horse's name?"

Lukas shot right back: "Don't worry. It'll be a household name by Saturday night."

On Saturday night the 30-1 Charismatic was indeed a household name and Ebanks was two thousand dollars poorer.

Now you know why I missed having Wayne Lukas in the 2001 Derby.

After the daily visit to Lukas' barn, I trudge along from barn to barn, with my tape recorder and notepad in hand, looking for interesting dialogue and anecdotes. When reporting this way, you must know when to use something and when not to. Although you're tempted to bring the reader deep into the trenches of the Derby, you must think of the ramifications of such an intrusion. That little tape recorder you're holding can be a deadly weapon if used irresponsibly. It's only after gaining the confidence and respect of trainers that they'll allow you behind closed doors with a tape recorder in your hand. I admit, however, sometimes they don't see it, so you have to be careful what you use. You don't want to write something that would jeopardize a trainer's job for the sake of getting some good quotes.

The second week is anything but peaceful, as the hordes of media pile in daily. I no longer am the public's main source of information. All the great human-interest stories I come across during the first week are now plastered all over newspapers across the country. I concentrate more on the works and my observations for the Bloodhorse.com web site, while saving most of the color for my recap story.

During Derby Week, the number of media is surpassed only by the number of doughnuts that pass through the door of the backstretch media center. The sound of pounding hooves on the track mingles with the chorus of slurps from hundreds of coffee cups. At night, room-service pizza is replaced by dinner at the Brown Hotel's English Grill with Joe Hirsch and friends or at Vincenzo's or John E's or Furlong's. Man, what a job!

There are no more exciting days leading up to the Derby than those when Bob Baffert works his Derby horse, or as is often the case with Lukas, his Derby horses. Between his pre-work quips, mixed with a case of nerves, his two-way radio conversations with the exercise rider, and his post-work one-liners, you're never at a loss for material.

In 1998 Baffert had Indian Charlie and Real Quiet

The two-way radio means business for Bob Baffert.

in the Derby. The horse Baffert feared the most was Event of the Year, trained by Jerry Hollendorfer and owned by one of Baffert's clients, John Mabee. The horse Mabee feared was Indian Charlie, and every time Baffert would work Indian Charlie, Mabee would call him from California, even though it was only a little after 5:30 back there. After Indian Charlie worked five furlongs one morning in a tame 1:01 4/5, Mabee called Baffert, who decided to do a little patronizing. "He went good, but he's no Event of the Year," he said with that Little Lord Fauntleroy grin of his. "Your horse is in a class of his own. But I don't mind running second to you."

Five days later Baffert sent Indian Charlie out for another work, and the Santa Anita Derby winner went in a blazing :58 4/5 for five furlongs, 1:11 1/5 for six furlongs, and galloping out seven furlongs in a sensational 1:24 1/5. "I think we just lost our price," Baffert said. A few minutes later, Mabee called, and this time Baffert gave it to him straight between the eyes. "You're in trouble," he said.

The following day Event of the Year fractured a knee during a work. As it turned out, Baffert's other horse, Real Quiet, won the Derby. Indian Charlie was third and never raced again.

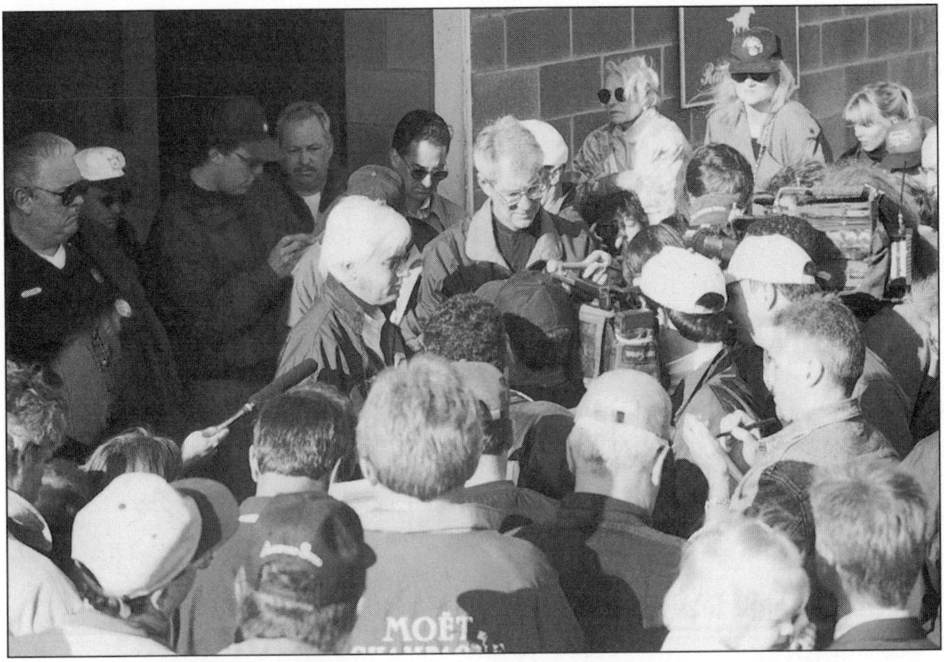

Baffert tantalizes the media with his quips and one-liners.

This is the same trainer, who before the 1997 Kentucky Derby, walked into a hair salon in Louisville with trainer Walter Greenman. With their identical white mops of hair, they looked like a pair of walking snow cones. The receptionist did quite a double take when these two ambled in the shop, then handed them information cards to fill out. Where it asked for occupation, Baffert wrote in "porn star." The look on the hair stylist's face when she came out to get her customer definitely was worth the proverbial thousand words.

Each trainer is an individual, and you have to accept his or her way of doing things. While most are great with their comments at any time, Neil Drysdale and Frank Brothers (who saddled Pulpit in 1997) would not talk to any member of the media until training hours were over. In 1967, well before my Derby assignments began, Frank Whiteley came to Louisville with the overwhelming favorite, Damascus. Whiteley was the quintessential hardboot and wanted nothing to do with the media. When Churchill Downs officials finally pleaded with Whiteley to talk to the press, he granted an interview outside his barn. The first question asked him was, "What are Damascus' sleeping habits?" Whiteley barked, "How the hell would I know, I never slept with him." End of interview.

Which brings us to the media — a composite creature that takes on many appearances. It can be as active as a chipmunk in late autumn or as inactive as a sloth hanging by its tail. Emanating from its thousands of brain cells come either pearls of knowledge and eloquence or a vacuous flow of verbal diarrhea.

To the credit of trainers, they must answer questions from the *Toledo Blade* and the *El Paso Times* with the same enthusiasm they do from *The New York*

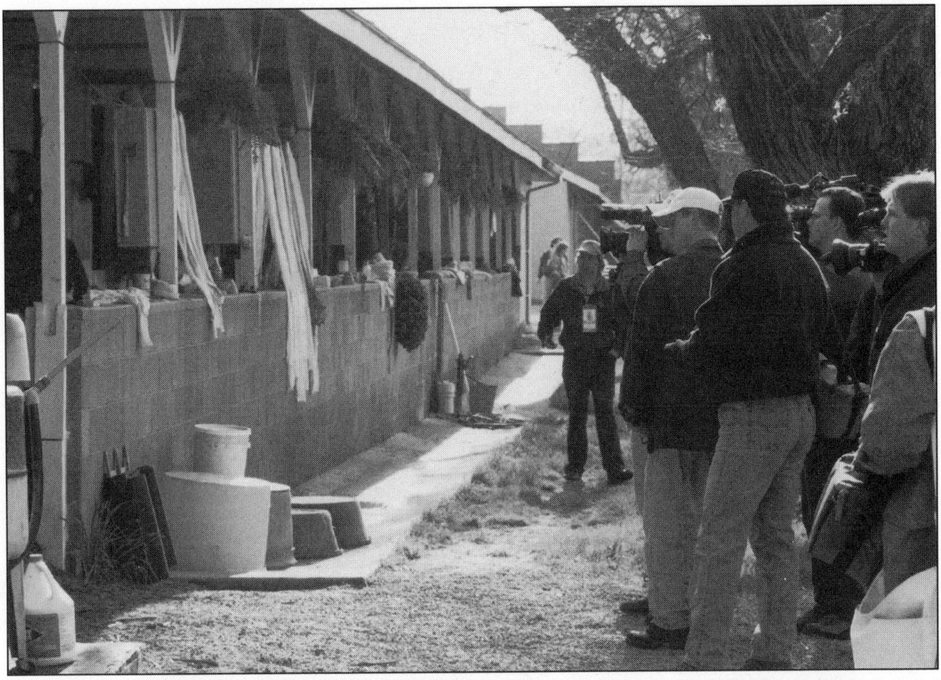

The media, author included (top left), wait for a glimpse of a Derby contender.

Times and the *Daily Racing Form*. Well, let's just say they're supposed to.

A reporter from a trade publication or a major newspaper can frown or even chuckle at the asinine questions from so-called gonzo journalists who are assigned to cover one race a year. Then again, he or she can enlighten these unfortunate, wayward souls, and help in any way to make their job a little easier. They just don't know any better than to ask, "So, what do you think of your horse's chances?" Part of

Charlie Whittingham didn't suffer fools gladly.

what separates the Derby from other races is the influx of reporters from small towns whose residents wouldn't know the difference between Belmont Park and Yellowstone Park.

And remember, we all have to start somewhere, and we all have had our moments. While I was covering the Preakness in 1994, someone had mentioned to me that they heard Charlie Whittingham was going to remove Numerous' blinkers. Although the colt had won the Derby Trial in his previous start, with blinkers on for the first time, he did show a tendency to throw his head in the air, indicating that perhaps the blinkers weren't doing their job. At the time, it made sense that Whittingham would feel the colt didn't need them. While Whittingham was being interviewed by a group of reporters, I launched a rocket of knowledge and wisdom right at him. "So Charlie, are you thinking of taking the blinkers off Numerous for the Preakness?" I asked, believing that I already knew the answer.

Whittingham slowly turned his bald head in my direction and stared at me for a second, which seemed like an eternity. "Why would I want to do that?" he asked. "Uh, duh, well, he does run with his head in the air," I blabbered. Then it hit me like a ton of bricks. At that agonizing moment in time, I was a gonzo journalist!

But more important, it was another lesson well learned. Don't try to impress anyone. Like spitting into the wind, it is inevitable that trying to impress someone will come back and hit you right in the face.

Here are the top ten ways of knowing if someone is a gonzo journalist:

10) He comes in late on a Neil Drysdale interview and asks him to repeat everything he missed.

9) He walks up to the security officer at Bob Baffert's barn at 6:30 in the morning and asks: "Is Bob here?"

8) He looks at Wayne Lukas' cowboy boots and tells him he bought the exact same pair on sale at Thom McAn.

7) He asks Nick Zito how come he's not in the Hall of Fame.

6) He spots Bobby Frankel having breakfast in the track kitchen and asks if he can join him.

5) He asks Prince Ahmed Salman if he would get special satisfaction in kicking Sheikh Mohammed's butt in the Derby.

4) In order to make a good impression, he shows up at Mary Lou Whitney's party with a box of assorted cookies and a bottle of Soave Bolla.

3) He has never heard of Joe Hirsch.

2) He is amazed how real the roses look on the victory blanket.

And the number one way of knowing if someone is a gonzo journalist:

He asks Charlie Whittingham if he's going to take the blinkers off his horse.

But with years comes wisdom. And with wisdom comes a comfort in who you are and how you go about your job. Ralph Waldo Emerson said, "The wise man is he who in the midst of the crowd keeps with perfect sweetness the independence of solitude." To me, the stories are where the crowds aren't. You just have to be confident enough in your own instincts. While hordes of journalists are huddled

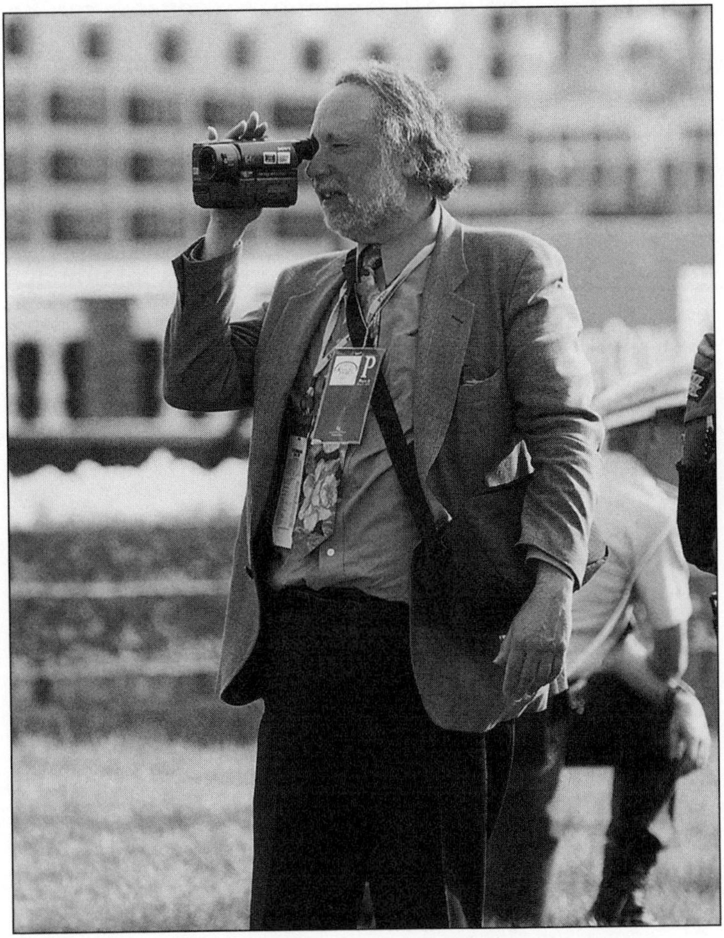

The author took more than notes in 2001.

around a trainer, all getting the same quotes, I head elsewhere. There are always stories floating around the Churchill Downs backstretch if you just go off and search for them. You'd be surprised how many great stories crop up while you're one on one with a trainer or an exercise rider or a groom or an assistant. The Baffert and Lukas and Zito quotes can be gotten any time, and their stock comments can be picked up off the press notes if that's what you desire. To journalists filing daily deadline stories, they are of great use. To me, dealing with a daily web site and a three-thousand-word recap for a weekly magazine, I have little use for press notes and am in constant search for color and human-interest stories. It is a luxury most beat journalists dealing with hard news don't have.

Every journalist at Churchill would love to get a scoop, but scoops are as rare as a Baffert horse working five furlongs in 1:03. There are simply too many insiders and good hard-nosed reporters on the Churchill backstretch Derby Week, and news travels very fast. If you do come across late-developing news, it is best to just share it with fellow journalists. Exclusives are not as important in the long run as developing trusting relationships.

You also have to know how to get information out of trainers. I recall one morning before the 1996 Derby when Bob Baffert, then a newcomer to the Derby, told me that Unbridled's Song, who shared his barn, was wearing bar shoes. Jennie Rees of the *Louisville Courier-Journal,* one of the most dedicated and hard-working Turf writers in the country, had also heard about it. We discussed the best way of broaching the subject to trainer Jim Ryerson, who was doing a TV interview at the time. We both went over to him and asked him a few standard questions, then looked at each other, as if, "Okay, now what?"

Knowing Ryerson pretty well, I just threw it right at him. "So, Jim, how long has Unbridled's Song been wearing bar shoes?" I blurted out. The smirk on Ryerson's face provided the confirmation. There's one rule I've discovered about information you're sure is almost one hundred-percent true and just need it confirmed. Don't ask about it. Talk about it as if it is common knowledge, but be pretty sure you're right. Anyone generally will discuss anything if he or she is sure you already know it for a fact to be true. For example: "Has Point Given been retired?" That's a no-no. "So, when did you make the decision to retire Point Given?" That's the right way. You have now taken away their option of giving some rhetorical, useless response, and forced them either to confirm it or tell you on the record that you're wrong. They know if they do the latter you can now portray them as a liar.

Logistics are also important in covering the Derby. While ninety-nine percent of the journalists stay on the backside during important works, I always drive through the infield tunnel to the frontside to watch the horses from the grandstand. Not only do you get a chance to see the works live, you can get great color hanging out with trainers who are there clocking their horses, many times with the owners. Baffert, with his stopwatch and two-way radio hookup with the exercise rider, always puts on a good show. This is priceless behind-the-scenes stuff that no one else will have. You do miss seeing the horses come off the track, which can be very revealing, but you have to make a choice. Some trainers never go to the frontside and are content just to see the work in bits and pieces, catching a glimpse of the horse on the frontside in between the giant tents set up in the infield.

And finally, what would the Kentucky Derby be without the celebrities? I am in no way star struck or enamored with movie stars, but the rest of the world

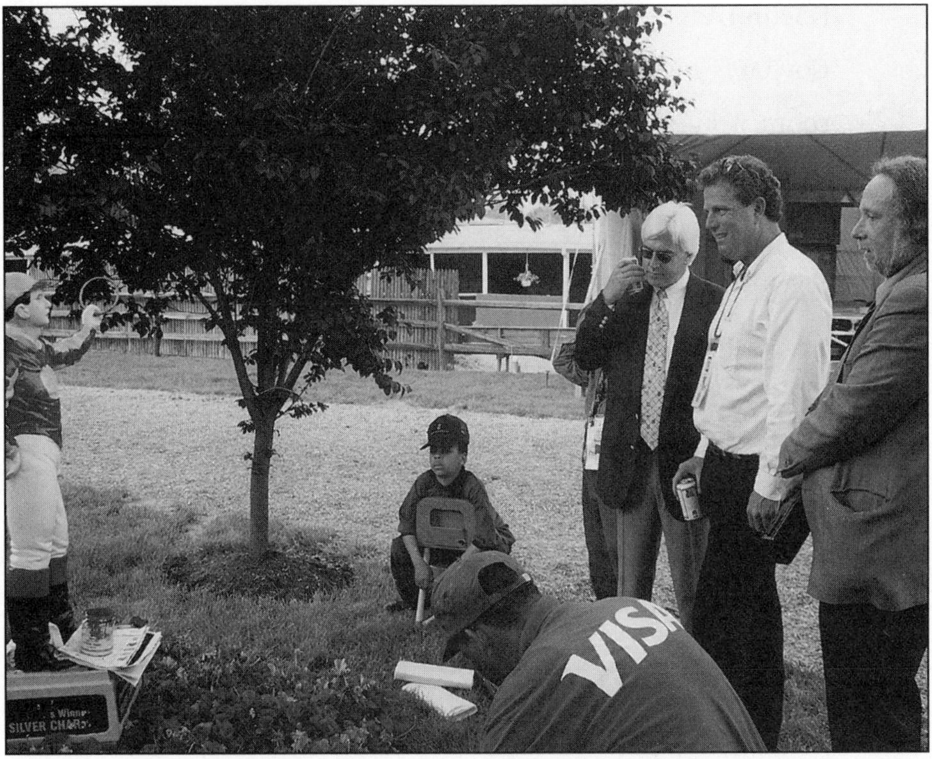

The author hanging out with Baffert and Pegram.

seems to be, and all I hear is, "You actually spoke to so-and-so?" One of my jobs after taking over *Daily Racing Form*'s "Derby Doings" from Joe Hirsch was to prowl the dining rooms and terraces and any other place where I could find celebrities and leading racing figures and put whatever I could into a Saturday notes column. I went through the motions for two years. I did manage to get quotes from numerous celebrities, but when I found myself talking to Kato

Kaelin (remember him?) and following former Dallas Cowboys head coach Jimmy Johnson into the men's room, I knew it was time to send this assignment to the great notes column in the sky.

So there it is. Two weeks of mostly cool, invigorating mornings; the golden sun illuminating a horse's mane and tail, as steam rises from its powerful flanks; gazing awestruck at the Twin Spires; seeing the best three-year-olds in the country close up every day until they become ingrained in the psyche; chatting with trainers and colleagues; dining at the finest restaurants for free; going to parties; walking from the barn area with the Derby horses; standing at the end of the tunnel as the horses and riders walk right by, while the strains of "My Old Kentucky Home" seem to pour down from the heavens. Yep, this is one rough assignment, but I guess like all tough jobs, someone's got to do it.

CHAPTER

Hope Springs Eternal

They charm, they tease, and they inspire dreams. Their allure is as strong as that of the most seductive siren. They are two-year-old Thoroughbreds. In the equine world there are no terrible twos. Every two-year-old is wonderful and terrific, talent oozing from every pore. When you look into their eyes, you swear you can see the Twin Spires as clearly as you would on a crisp May morning. There is an old racetrack saying that goes: no one with a two-year-old in his barn ever committed suicide.

It's okay to gaze into a two-year-old's eyes, as long as you're prepared for the magical images in there to fade. Some last longer than others, and one will never fade. That one is what keeps owners and trainers living in hope. If it can happen to Dennis Diaz, Pedro Baptista, Jack and Katherine Price, Karen and Mickey Taylor, and Jim and Sally Hill, it can happen to anyone. The odds of winning the Kentucky Derby in a particular year are infinitely better than hitting the lottery, and the challenge is more stimulating than going to your neighborhood luncheonette and filling in a bunch of numbers on a card.

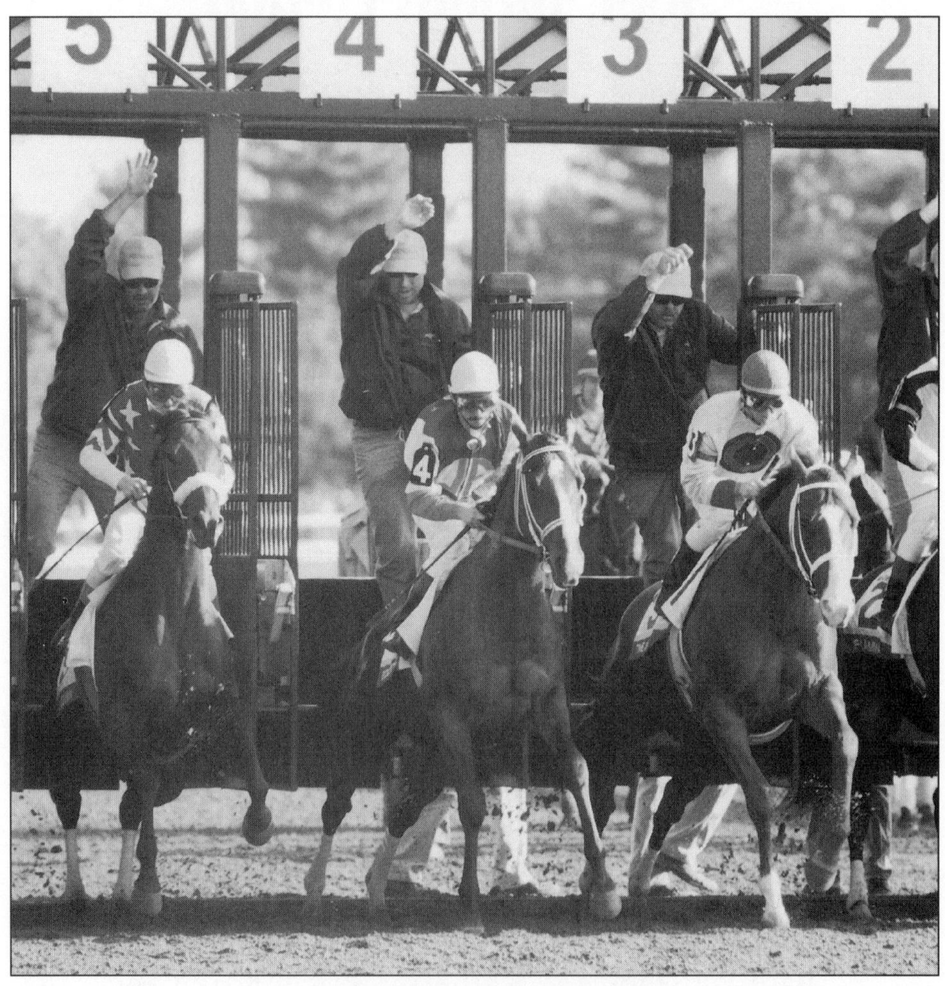

When two-year-old racing begins each spring, everyone has a chance of winning the Derby.

As a two-year-old, Seattle Slew was known as "Baby Huey."

When two-year-old racing begins each spring, all trainers start from scratch. The playing field is level, and hopes abound. Sure, you have two-million-dollar yearlings and two-year-old purchases competing against bargain-basement youngsters, but we've already established that all the money in the world will not buy you a Derby winner. Everyone at this time of the year has a chance at immortality.

If there is one thing all two-year-olds have in common, it's that they have a remarkable knack for disguise. We see tortoise-like horses masquerading as champions, and we see Triple Crown winners masquerading as tortoises. When Seattle Slew was a young two-year-old, he was nicknamed "Baby Huey," after the gawky cartoon character. His co-owner Jim Hill described him as a "big, clumsy-galloping horse." Secretariat was big, fat, and awkward when trainer Lucien Laurin first laid eyes on him, and the colt couldn't finish within fifteen lengths of his workmates. Laurin knew Secretariat wouldn't show anything on the track until the youngster got rid of his baby fat and learned what being a racehorse was all about.

Derby prognostication at this time is nearly impossi-

Summer Squall won the Hopeful Stakes at two.

ble. If you had asked Wayne Lukas where he would have ranked Charismatic on his list of Derby hopefuls, you can bet Lukas would have placed the son of Summer Squall down at the bottom. And where do you think Bob Baffert would have ranked the narrowly built, crooked-legged Real Quiet after the colt finished a well-beaten seventh in his career debut, then went on to be beaten twice at Santa Fe Downs in New Mexico before finally breaking his maiden in his seventh start?

You can get an idea of how far two-year-olds might want to run by studying their pedigree, and you can tell how precocious they are by the speed they display in their early training. But these little kids are a long way from adulthood, and a world of potential still awaits them. As summer spills into autumn, the signs begin to appear. Do they have good minds, or are they still green and goofy? Do they relish a brawl, or do they back away when someone looks them in the eye?

By autumn a two-year-old probably has raced a time or two, and its owner and trainer have some kind of idea of its potential. As is the case with many two-year-olds, though, injuries can derail the training schedule. Young horse ailments include bucked shins, sore splint bones (both of which affect the cannon bone), and ankle and knee chips. Some horses have chips removed by surgery, while others continue to race with them. It all depends on the severity, the number of chips, and the advice of the veterinarian. Fusaichi Pegasus had a chip removed at two, while an iron horse like Skip Away raced his entire career with an ankle chip. Early in his two-year-old season, Monarchos developed sore shins and an abscess on one of his feet.

As always, trends can be helpful in forming the ultimate portrait of a Derby winner. Be wary, however. They do change.

Of the past thirty Derby winners, twenty-two made their first start between June 9 and September 30. Only one — Fusaichi Pegasus — made his first start later than October. Fusaichi's actually came on December 11. But here we go with trend changes again. From 1970 to 1999, no Derby winner failed to break his or her maiden as a two-year-old. But the last two Derby winners — Monarchos and Fusaichi Pegasus — broke their maidens in January of their three-year-old campaign. Could it be merely a coincidence, considering their respective trainers — John Ward Jr. and Neil Drysdale — are known for their conservative approach? Or are we witnessing the beginning of a new trend where conservative is now the way to go?

The 1978 Derby winner Affirmed won his career debut.

We are throwing out all these scenarios, not to confuse, but to take a devil's advocate approach to trends. Don't take them too seriously, especially with two-year-olds.

One trend that has changed dramatically over the years is the number of starts it takes a future Derby winner to break his maiden. Over an eleven-year period, from 1974 to 1984, eight future Derby winners broke their maidens in their career debut. Six of them came in consecutive years — Foolish Pleasure in 1974,

Bold Forbes in '75, Seattle Slew in '76, Affirmed in '77, Spectacular Bid in '78, and Genuine Risk in '79.

In the last eleven years, however, only one future Derby winner — Grindstone — won his career debut. Monarchos, Go for Gin, and Strike the Gold took three starts; Sea Hero, four; Charismatic, six; and Real Quiet, seven.

We are seeing more and more maiden races dominated by horses with speed-oriented pedigrees, so young classic-type horses have it a little tougher getting through those five- and five-and-a-half-furlong races. Even a great barometer like the Hopeful Stakes no longer provides the clear look into the future it once did. The crowning event for two-year-olds at Saratoga has been won by classic horses such as Secretariat, Affirmed, Native Dancer, Nashua, Whirlaway, Jaipur, and, yes, even Man o' War. But in recent years, it has been won by future sprinters and milers like City Zip, Yonaguska, Favorite Trick, Smoke Glacken, Wild Escapade, Great Navigator, Salt Lake, and Deposit Ticket. The last Kentucky Derby winner to capture the Hopeful was Affirmed in 1977. Since 1989, when Summer Squall won the Hopeful before winning the Preakness the following year, only two winners of the race — Favorite Trick and High Yield — have even run in a Triple Crown race.

I use the Hopeful as an indicator of how two-year-old racing has changed. The race is now seven furlongs, instead of its former distance of six and a half furlongs, and is run in September, instead of August. Still, our classic colts are not ready to compete in it. The Breeders' Cup World Thoroughbred Championships has thrown everything out of whack, and the bottom line is, you can take the two-year-old stakes season and basically toss it. There is no rhyme or reason to it any longer. It is a helter-skelter five or six months, with all types of horses coming from every nook and cranny around the country to try to make a name for themselves while they can. Now, in the summer and even early fall, when you hear a trainer use that old cliché, "I have a better one in the barn," chances are he does.

In short, you can look into a two-year-old's eyes and still dream. Just don't confuse what you're seeing with the hard reality that is the Kentucky Derby.

Photo Credits

Introduction: Skip Dickstein, p. 9; Mike Marten, p. 11; Barbara D. Livingston, p. 12

Chapter 1: Milt Toby, p. 21; Barbara D. Livingston, p. 23, 25, 27

Chapter 2: Anne M. Eberhardt, p. 32, 33; Ken Weaver, p. 34; Rick Samuels, p. 37; Keeneland-Cook, p. 39; Skip Dickstein, Barbara D. Livingston p. 42

Chapter 3: Barbara D. Livington, p. 46, 48, 50; Skip Dickstein, p. 49; Anne M. Eberhardt, p. 52, 56

Chapter 4: Anne M. Eberhardt, p. 60, 70; Barbara D. Livingston, p. 63, 73; Skip Dickstein, p. 67, 77, 79

Chapter 5: Barbara D. Livingston, p. 82, 91-92; Shigeki Kikkawa, p. 84; Skip Dickstein, p. 86; Anne M. Eberhardt, p. 87-88

Chapter 6: Anne M. Eberhardt, p. 97, 104; Barbara D. Livingston, p. 99, 101, 103

Chapter 7: Barbara D. Livingston, p. 109-110, 116; Anne M. Eberhardt, p. 112, 114, 119, 124; Rick Rickman, p. 123

Chapter 8: Belmont News Bureau, p. 129; Anne M. Eberhardt, p. 131, 137; Skip Dickstein, p. 134, 136

Chapter 9: Skip Ball, p. 143; Barbara D. Livingston, p. 146; Joy B. Gilbert, p. 148; The Blood-Horse, p. 152

Chapter 10: Barbara D. Livingston, p. 157; Kinetic Corporation, p. 161

Chapter 11: Shigeki Kikkawa, p. 171; Barbara D. Livingston, p. 173; Skip Dickstein, p. 178; Anne M. Eberhardt, p. 179

Chapter 13: Barbara D. Livingston, p. 191, 197, 199; Anne M. Eberhardt, p. 201, 205; Skip Dickstein, p. 202; The Blood-Horse, p. 209

Chapter 14: Anne M. Eberhardt, p. 212; NYRA Photo, p. 213, 217; The Blood-Horse, p. 214

About the Author

Steve Haskin is an award-winning Turf writer renowned for his Kentucky Derby commentary. During his nearly three decades at *Daily Racing Form*, Haskin made a name with his "Derby Watch" columns. He joined *The Blood-Horse* magazine in 1998, and as senior correspondent provides coverage of the Triple Crown races and the Breeders' Cup. He has won three Red Smith Awards for his Kentucky Derby coverage.

Haskin has written three other books for Eclipse Press, including *Baffert: Dirt Road to the Derby*, co-authored with Derby-winning trainer Bob Baffert, and he has contributed to several other books published in the United States, England, and France.

Haskin, who also is editor of the *Kentucky Derby* and *Breeders' Cup* souvenir magazines, lives in Hamilton Square, New Jersey, with his wife and daughter.

Other Titles *from* ECLIPSE PRESS

At the Wire
Horse Racing's Greatest Moments

Baffert
Dirt Road to the Derby

Cigar
America's Horse (revised edition)

Country Life Diary
(revised edition)

Crown Jewels of Thoroughbred Racing

Dynasties
Great Thoroughbred Stallions

Etched in Stone

Four Seasons of Racing

Great Horse Racing Mysteries

Hoofprints in the Sand
Wild Horses of the Atlantic Coast

Investing in Thoroughbreds
Strategies for Success

Lightning in a Jar
Catching Racing Fever

Matriarchs
Great Mares of the 20th Century

Olympic Equestrian

Royal Blood

Thoroughbred Champions
Top 100 Racehorses of the 20th Century

Women in Racing
In Their Own Words

Affirmed and Alydar

Citation

Dr. Fager

Forego

Go for Wand

John Henry

Man o' War

Nashua

Native Dancer

Personal Ensign

Ruffian

Seattle Slew

Spectacular Bid

Sunday Silence

Swaps